Pieces of Me

PAUL SANCHEZ

Threadhead Records

Pieces of Me

Copyright © 2009 by Paul Sanchez Music LLC/Threadhead Records.

All rights reserved. No part of this book may be used or reproduced in any manner whatsoever without written permission except in the case of brief quotations embodied in critical articles and reviews. For information contact Threadhead Records, 11849 Olympic Boulevard, Suite 101, Los Angeles, CA 90064. (310) 733-7062.

First Edition April 2009

Edited by Chris Joseph, Tanya Younger, Heather McCamey, Michael Bailey and Colman deKay.

Photographs courtesy Jim Brock Photography © 2009, Mark 'Swag' Rosenzweig, Jeffrey Potter, Dennis Gardner, Nunu, Robert Alves, Shelly Sanchez, Robbie Moore and Ethel Moore.

ISBN 978-0-615-28014-1

Paul Sanchez

www.paulsanchez.com || www.myspace.com/paulpoppysanchez

Threadhead Records is an unprecedented non-profit record company formed out of the love for New Orleans, its music, and its musicians. Our mission is to help New Orleans musicians who were victims of the flooding that occurred from the failed levees in the wake of Hurricane Katrina. To this day, most of the musicians in New Orleans are still attempting to rebuild their lives.

Each CD project is funded by the fans themselves and is paid back by the musicians with an additional 10% charitable return to the New Orleans Musicians Clinic. The musicians own their own work; Threadhead Records does not sign artists, nor are we involved in creative decisions or ownership of songs. We exist solely to help musicians get their CDs made. No more, no less.

Threadhead Records is a way for Louisiana-based musicians to continue to produce the music they crave to create and, in return, gives their fans the music they love to hear. It's a truly wonderful partnership.

Please help us rebuild New Orleans, one song at a time.

For information, to order CDs and to contribute to Threadhead records visit:

www.threadheadrecords.com

"words lead to deeds...
    they prepare the soul, make it ready and move it to tenderness"

Ward No. 6, A. Chekov

All of my words, breath, life and love to Shelly.

Foreword

"Home is the place where, when you have to go there, they have to take you in."

Robert Frost

On the 30th of August in 2005, I bet there were thousands of New Orleanians who wanted to say, "Yea, you wrong, Mr. Frost."

As we approach the fourth anniversary of Hurricane Katrina, I often wonder, as I hope millions of others often wonder, how are all those amazing people who lost their homes and their lives? Have they found a place to live? Have they started over? Are they comfortable? Are they with their loved ones? Are they warm? Do they still have the will to live? (As you know, soon after, many did not.) I do hope that there are millions with this on their minds. It doesn't have to be at the forefront. I'd be satisfied with placement in their Top Ten. Some days, it feels like it's not even as important as "American Idol."

Paul Sanchez knows what it's like to be away from home. When you're a working musician, home is often anywhere you lay your hat. You deal with cold motel rooms, cold food, and cold people. You deal with it because you know that eventually the warmth of your family and your friends and your own bed are always waiting for you.

Almost always.

Paul was on tour when that bitch of a storm came barreling through New Orleans in August of 2005. Paul watched in horror when the levees broke, and flooded his city. We all did. But when the majority of us had seen enough, and we settled in with a cup of tea and a Seinfeld rerun at the end of our day, Paul did not. Paul could not. Not his choice. When we woke up a few days later and put on a pot of coffee, made some breakfast, and got the kids off to school, we forgot temporarily, that arguably the greatest city in all of America was under water. We forgot because we didn't experience it, therefore, it doesn't exist.

I spoke to a good friend of mine on September 12, 2001. I live in NYC. He lives in Los Angeles. The afternoon of September 12, 2001, not a full day after the worst terror attack on American soil, my friend put me on hold as I was telling my 9/11 story. He "didn't realize it was STILL that bad in New York." 24 hours later and he didn't "realize." He's a pretty smart guy and I love him. But COME ON! My friend wasn't here. I gave him some slack. And we weren't there, in New Orleans. It's easy to forget. Just not for the good, innocent people of New Orleans.

Paul hasn't forgotten.

What follows is one man's agony and confusion. His sadness. His loss. His denial and his acceptance. His will to take back his life, no matter how unrecognizable. Writes Paul:

> *"I sat in an alley crying for New Orleans, its abandoned poor, the chaos and the innocent victims in its path. I noticed through my tears that I was sitting in a pattern of light, rectangles through the windows of an office building. The rectangles lead my eyes finally to the corner of the building then out to beautiful, pure sunlight and I remembered that light and love wait beyond these sad shadows."*

WE SHOULD NOT TOSS NEW ORLEANS ASIDE. THINGS ARE NOT OKAY.

Things are better, just not okay.

This is Paul Sanchez "unplugged." Don't put him on hold. Please.

Sal Nunziato, Huffington Post
burnwoodtonite.blogspot.com
February 2009

What I lost in the flood was my stuff – what I have found since then is my life.
Paul Joseph Sanchez

Prologue

April 2009

Pieces of Me

In November of 2006 I changed my life, or rather I accepted that my life had been changed.

New Orleans had flooded a year and three months before. My wife Shelly and I were on the road with Cowboy Mouth, the band we had traveled with for over a decade, when it happened. We watched, like thousands of others, as our homes and lives vanished under the flood waters.

For the first few months after the flood we wandered the country with the band and then went to England and Amsterdam for a while, just running, not facing choices or reality, and most certainly not dealing with the future. The future, however, has a way of insisting that you get on with life, and events unfolded that led me to do so.

I had reached the end of the road professionally, emotionally, spiritually and physically. Having just started to learn how to use a computer and not knowing much of anything about the internet, my friend and band mate Sonia Tetlow showed me how to blog, and that was how I began to learn, through writing blogs. I didn't know who I was writing to, but it was an outlet for feelings, thoughts, questions and answers; and I wrote as if I were writing to my best friend. In the end I suppose I was writing to me.

Reading them now, I wince at how emotionally raw and openly vulnerable I was at the time, so much more lost than I knew. I was reliving my own journey out of the wilderness of disconnection and back to the land of life and living. I've done a bit of work to shape them from blogs and into stories, but in many cases, knowing that I couldn't duplicate the feelings of the moment, I have left them as they were.

I blogged hoping that other folks who were as lost as I was would read them and not feel so alone. I also wrote them because I was scared and felt very alone, and having these words out in the world made me feel like someone was listening and cared. They made me feel connected.

When Tanya Younger and Chris Joseph of Threadhead Records contacted me and asked if I'd be interested in turning the blogs into stories for a book, my first thought was who, besides me, would be interested? I agreed because I thought it would be a gas to have a book out. Ultimately though it was for the same reason I wrote them. This is two years of my life. Hoping, stumbling, working, falling and getting back up.

I send it out into the world, and hope that someone who is out there stumbling themselves might read these stories and know that all of us fall down sometimes, and that there is a tomorrow.

August 2006

Coming Home

After the flood, we were home off and on from December 2005 until Jazz Fest in April 2006.

Long enough to get an apartment on Royal Street, long enough for some pain to work its way through the numbness, long enough to hug what friends had made their way back to the city, to hear some music, eat some food, long enough to remember where we were from and why we love it.

Looking back it seems like a sweet lifetime ago.

Shelly and I got the place on Royal in February 2006. We had been staying, one could say overstaying, at the home of our friends Tom and Sandi, one block down on Royal, since we got back to New Orleans in December. They had offered us their place for a few weeks when we got back to New Orleans, and we were so frozen in shock that we just stayed, put off making a move or a choice of any kind about anything. As we were tip-toeing back to life, we just got an apartment close to where we'd landed.

It has been a lovely and re-affirming experience. Boutté rides by in the mornings on his bike and gives his familiar little bird call if our balcony windows are open to see if we want to have a coffee. We are above Fifi Mahoney's Wig Shop. You have to walk through the store to get to our stairway, which is surreal enough when the store is open in the day time, but in the evenings when closed it is ridiculously, laughably, perfect.

This is how we have come back to New Orleans. We wake up and just watch life unfold on Royal Street, sitting on our balcony, from the sweet to the surreal. The city is still very empty; it is odd and sad, but at the same time we have it to ourselves for a while as we try to figure out what it is we have. Trust me; you have to really want to live in New Orleans to be here now. There is a sweetness and a feeling of ownership to the emptiness, a feeling of safety. We walk or ride bikes at all hours of the night without a thought to safety. Who is here to rob you and what does anyone have to steal? Still, there are hours to spend visiting on the balcony with friends new and old. Boutté's voice sings from the balcony and calls out to everyone on the streets below, whether he knows them or not, and somehow the fact that he so clearly belongs in New Orleans makes me feel as if I surely must.

We left New Orleans in June 2006 for Cowboy Mouth's summer tour and were gone for two months. We kept busy trying to help friends and family, trying to explain to folks around the country what was going on back home, trying to not think about what was, and what lay ahead. It was good to sing and be with people who wanted to help when hugging us was the only help they had to give and when being hugged meant more than we knew then or have remembered since. I didn't want to think about what was coming next and couldn't have seen it coming – literally.

The Mouth was playing Chicago in July at Sheffield Garden Walk. It was a lovely neighborhood event held during that six week stretch when the weather in Chicago is gorgeous. There are block parties and bands, and we had played it for a few years. I had done sound check and was riding my bike back to the hotel to relax. I had hours before the show, and Chicago is one of my favorite cities in the country for riding a bike because they have a lot of bikers, bike lanes and bike conscious drivers, usually.

I was rounding a corner near a hotel by Lincoln Park and a taxi was double parked outside the hotel. It wasn't too busy traffic-wise so I eased into the next lane and started to go around him. Just as I went past, the driver door flew open with enough time for me to see it as I hit it. Next thing I know, he flips, he flies, he falls, he lands. I went head over heels leaving the bike smashed into the driver door. I landed on my back and head in front of the cab. I staggered to my feet and looked at my crumpled bike. The taxi driver walked up and asked if I was okay....being in shock, I said I was going to walk to my hotel and leave my bike because it didn't look like it would work. He said if I was alright he was going to leave, and, still not knowing how bad I looked or what I was doing, I said yes, I would walk.

As he jumped in his cab to leave, some folks standing outside the hotel stopped him and told me I was probably hurt more than I realized. I remember saying I was alright over and over and then I remember getting over-heated and everything started to go dark. I tried to sit down as fast as I could but woke up face down in a

Chicago gutter. I sat up, threw up, and announced to the stunned passers-by that I felt better and was leaving. A nice young hippy boy whose name I never got, grabbed my shoulder and said softly, "Man, you're not going anywhere. I already called an ambulance. Look at your face." He held up a mirror and my face was dirty and bruised. I got a little shaky and managed to grab my cell to call Shelly and let her know what was happening and where I was. Being Shelly she ran from stage set up and was going to ride her bike to the scene when some cops saw the state she was in. She told them what was up and wound up getting a lift to the scene in a police car just as I was being put in the ambulance. The doctors were cool, they ran what tests they had to while I kept insisting I had to get out and play that show at Sheffield Garden Walk. I was hit around three and played the show at seven that evening. I don't remember the show or the next couple of days very well, but my photographer friend, Nunu, was there and I have pictures.

Suddenly the world came to a halt, the tour was over, the running from New Orleans was done.

Coming home has been jarring. After two months of being in cities and towns that function and are alive, I'm stunned to be back in New Orleans where the heat of August and the inertia of government just makes you furious. It seems like you and everyone you know wakes up sad and just gets sadder. For a mood change we flip to angry and frustrated, but really, it's too hot and I'm too tired for anger.

When the 'Thing', as Times Picayune writer Chris Rose dubbed it, happened it was painful, but we all thought "When this pain ends I'll get back to my life." Now we know we can never have our old lives back. For those of us who lost houses and neighborhoods, whose families and friends are scattered across the country, we can go on to new lives, but the familiarity of who we were is gone. The streets seem dirtier, the people more desperate, and all of us move as if we are still under water. The hope comes from other people, people I know but mostly people I don't.

My own house was gutted by a group called Arabi Wrecking Krewe, a group of musicians and music fans who volunteer to gut the homes of musicians. By August 2006 they had gutted over eighty homes. They came to my house and hauled out our ruined stuff that had sat for weeks in the flooded toxic soup our neighborhood had become.

These strangers from across the country did work that would have made me vomit and weep. Did so with grace and humor. Stepped back to give my wife and me a moment to cry for our lost memories. I bought them po' boys for lunch along with a portable radio so they could listen to WWOZ, and they thanked me as if I was doing them a favor. After lunch, bowling in the middle of the street with their empty water bottles and my old bowling ball, they were like kids having a laugh, but they are heroes to me. The kind of heroes the city is going to need thousands of to continue to rebuild. The kind of heroes who nobody sees on the news, nobody pays money to. They do it to give something back to New Orleans music, and for me they did much more. They gave me hope when I wanted to give up. They reminded me that good folks doing good things starts with individuals.

I truly can't repay them for what they did for me, but if you read this and want to help New Orleans in some small way, write to them as a fan of New Orleans music and say thank you. They work on their days off, and the musicians are up until three in the morning playing and then gutting homes by eight a.m. Long, dirty, hot hours because they want to give back. Drop a line and say thanks to some beautiful people.

Spread the word. New Orleans will be saved one person at a time... one song at a time.

Shelly and me in front of Fifi Mahoney's Wig Shop

November 2006

Reminded Me of Leaving

Seventeen years ago I was working on movies in New Orleans, Boston, New York and Los Angeles. Rolling cable, drinking and wishing I was playing music for a living. I used to bring my guitar to the set and would spend as much time playing as I did working, which you would think would really piss off the people who were really busting hump, but they seemed to like it. I think folks knew I wasn't destined for a career in film and encouraged me to go on singing. Either that or I was so incredibly inept at my job that me singing was at least me safely out of the way of the actual process of film making.

Then I got a call from my old friends in New Orleans, Fred and Griff, asking if I wanted to be in a band. That band became Cowboy Mouth, and it was sixteen years of the most fun and adventure a man could want. We played great shows. Our motto was always, "Ten or ten thousand, we give 'em our best," and for sixteen years we tried to. The flood seemed to bring us together musically and as friends like we hadn't been in years.

In October 2006 the band's lawyer asked to take me to lunch, and since he was and is a friend, I thought it was just for fun. He took me to a very nice place to tell me that Griff and Fred wanted an ex-manager, one I did not want to work with, back. Since they both knew I wasn't comfortable working with this guy, in fact I had made it plain that I didn't want to work with him again, and since they had asked our lawyer to take me to lunch and tell me they wanted him back as manager when either of them could have leaned across the aisle of the bus in any of the countless hours we spent on the road together to tell me, I assumed they would rather risk alienating me then pass up the chance to work with him again. I tried for a while after that to make it work but whatever bond might have existed vanished in our new business set-up.

I was so tired of running. Tired of trying to be something the Mouth needed, instead of who I wanted to be. My body still reverberated with pain from the accident in Chicago. I was tired of the uncertainty. Life had suddenly become very uncertain, and I asked myself if I was doing what I really wanted with my music in my time on the planet. I realized there was so much more I wanted for my songs and for me.

There was more to my leaving the band, there always is with bands, but it's all been said before. Picture the Beatles with no fame or money or any VH1 Behind the Music, without the platinum records and arenas full of fans. Shortly after the ex-manager's return he informed Shelly, who was working as our co-road manager, that she would be the first in the organization asked to take a pay cut. Being the only female in our employ she was expecting this. In fact, a very similar situation had occurred the last time he managed us. She had not had a raise or a bonus in years and was already being paid less than our last two tour mangers. Shelly had enjoyed working with the band even less then I had the last time around with this guy at the wheel, so she quit rather than take a pay cut and work with the kind of vibe the band was headed toward.

I watched it unfold, knowing it was coming, but not thinking it would happen. I tried to call Fred to see if he would help but he only texted back, "Talk to the manager." I sat in the back of the bus watching Shelly pack up her belongings to leave, remembering the last time she had left the road and what a drag it all was without her to share it with. I was thinking to myself, "I can't believe I'm watching her pull away again", then said it out loud, "I can't believe I'm watching her pull away again." Then I looked at Sonia, who was sitting in the back lounge of the bus with me and said, "I'm not watching her pull away again. I quit." I texted Fred back and told him to replace me.

The flooding of New Orleans has changed all our lives and forced us to change direction. A friend of mine from Indianapolis said to me, "You can be a better man or a worse man but you can't be the same man." That's it really. There are many reasons why I left, but I simply wasn't the same man and had to find out what kind of man I would be.

When my brother Andrew, who taught me to play guitar, died, Fred and Griff were there for me. When my mom and Fred's mom died, Fred and I could look at each other across the bus without speaking and know how the other guy felt, rolling along the highway with a broken heart. When New Orleans flooded and Shelly and I lost our home, Griff comforted us, even as he endured the loss of his mother and his marriage.

We endured egos, business pressures, managers trying to tear us apart and the road itself. We were there for each other as family members and brothers in arms for sixteen years (and even real brothers don't always like each other).

I thank Griff, Fred, Sonia, Mary, Rob, Steve and Clem for their part in building the Mouth. I thank all the guys who worked with us and for us. I thank Maw-maw who did our merchandise mail outs well into her eighties and would still be doing them if the flooding hadn't taken her home.

Mostly, I thank my wife Shelly for doing everything she could in her twelve years with the band to help keep us on the road. She borrowed thousands of dollars from her parents to start a merchandise company for the band when we didn't have the money to do it ourselves. She drove the all night shifts when we were still in vans. She loaded gear when the clubs didn't provide loaders, refusing to let the band help so we wouldn't risk getting our hands hurt pre-show. Eventually, she became tour manager because we were in financial trouble and needed someone we could trust. She worked from the time the bus rolled into town at dawn until the bus rolled out of town at three a.m. the next day. While we played, partied, slept, and asked for more, she worked. She is my hero.

I wish the Mouth all the success they deserve. I'm pleased that the Cowboy Mouth I played in ended up feeling like a family that looked out for each other as we fought with each other, laughed with each other and rocked together. When we dug it and even when we didn't. In wishing the band well in their new direction, I will take my wife's hand and follow love's path where it takes us. It has always been my dream to strum and sing and tell stories to a room full of folks who want a real human moment.

I believe in my heart I will find that audience. Keep listening for me, my heart is full with songs, and my head is bursting with stories to tell.

See you down the road.

December 2006

Escape to Belize

If you ever need a place to go for a few weeks to recharge your spirit, be alone with someone you love and plan a new life, I highly recommend San Pedro, Belize. The people are lovely, with friendly smiling faces and a 'hello' from everyone you meet. No cars on the Island; golf carts and bicycles are the mode of transportation, and I like any place where I can get around by bike. It's sort of like New Orleans with an ocean. Waking up to beautiful sunrises over the ocean and dreaming of new possibilities.

Our hosts at El Pescador have been the most generous and kind people. They have given us compassion, wisdom, and space to be and decide. Shelly and I, like most folks who lost everything in the flood, have been in shock, reeling and frozen in time since then. This place, and the peace that exists for the people that live here, has given us a chance to catch our breath, to hold on to each other and find the will to move forward again with our lives.

I won't say I'm not anxious, because it's difficult to make a living as a professional musician. But what are we if we don't face the unknown in life, the things we fear that challenge our being? We become spectators in our own lives if we don't reach for new horizons.

So, nervous and hopeful I make the plunge into the unknown.

Shelly talked me into scuba diving. I'm afraid of the water and afraid of sharks, but it was the unknown and we jumped in. Once I remembered to relax and breathe, I found myself in a whole new world that I'd never dreamt existed. Swimming with sharks (real ones not the dangerous ones in the music business) and swimming with a huge stingray circling us, let us know that we were visitors there at its discretion. Thousands of fish swimming all around us. So much life I never knew existed. I faced the unknown and found it frightening, exhilarating and beautiful beyond what I imagined.

Here's to dreaming good dreams and watching them come true.

A little girl dancing in the streets of San Pedro

January 2007

The More Things Change the More They Stay the Same

Back in New Orleans, I spent New Year's Eve at my brother John's house. He lives in a neighborhood that we both spent a good deal of time living in over the last few decades and has his party every year. I know the people. They are my old friends as well. There is a bonfire on the neutral ground across from his house and it is quite something at midnight. Fireworks, flames, a sense of danger and somehow romance in the air. I hadn't made his party much over the last sixteen years because my old job kept me busy most of the time, and almost always on New Year's Eve. Thirty-five hundred shows later it was nice to be with old friends. I got a lot of love that night from people whose lives I hadn't been very present in for a long time, although it seems like I was present in theirs more than I knew. It feels like the universe is sending folks to let me know that they love me and are as excited for my new direction in life as I am. It is humbling to remember how much my songs have been able to keep playing my life for me while I've been gone.

How do you say thanks for believing in me when I sometimes didn't know what it was I believed in myself?

I'm playing a show at d.b.a. in New Orleans early in 2007 and of the thousands of shows and the tens of thousands of people I've had a chance to sing and play for, I'm as excited by this show as any I've played.

It's where I've seen John Boutté create music and magic at his shows when I've been in town over the last several years. In fact, John got me the gig by telling one of the owners that he would be "a damned fool" not to have me play there. I always tell folks that ask how I started playing regular shows at d.b.a. that I paid my dues for fifteen years on the road in a rock band, made ten records with them (three of them on major labels), made nine solo records, and then John Boutté told them to book me so they did.

After the show Shelly and I will be flying back to Belize to live for a while. I need to get out of New Orleans. The devastation of my home and neighborhood still fills me with sadness. My friends who live here carry sadness like an extra suit made of skin, and anger is what keeps them going some days. I'm emotionally exhausted and looking forward to the peaceful life we'd found down in San Pedro. We are keeping our land in New Orleans, but didn't know if our neighborhood was coming back, and like so many other folks we wait.

In leaving for a while I hope to lose myself, to find my way home. I'm leaving to recharge, to have some peace, to find direction like thousands of folks who lost everything in the flood. We are not giving up on life or New Orleans. Instead, I hope to find a new path to the waterfall. I don't see myself as hero or a martyr, a saint or a sinner, and I don't see the folks who are staying in New Orleans as either. We are survivors trying to make our way through a landscape the likes of which we could not have imagined.

The heroes are the ones who stayed in New Orleans and pulled people out of their flooded homes. Thousands of stories you will never hear of neighbor helping neighbor, strangers helping strangers. The ones who brought food and water, gutted homes and gave up time from their lives to help folks they will never meet.

The real martyrs are the ones shot and killed in the days after, beaten and forgotten. Homeless and hungry for a nation to watch on CNN for a while, and then go back to watching American Idol. The poorest musicians in town wanting to stick it out in a city that loves them, but will not house them, even in the Musicians Village, the place where the completed home of a young musician friend of mine sits waiting for power to be turned on so he and his six year old son can have a home again, while the city keeps saying maybe next month or the month after that. Where a young man like Dinneral Shavers, who not only played drums for the Hot Eight Brass Band, but was a high school music teacher passing on a tradition to a generation that can only hope to be welcomed back to the new New Orleans, is gunned down in front of his family as violent crime continues and leadership lies waiting to blossom somewhere.

The Road Home program has had eighty-nine thousand applications. Shelly and I are in that number. As I write, of the billions of dollars that sit waiting to change people's lives, eighty families have been approved.

We all talk about one day.

One day my wife and I will live on an island.

One day I'll be a singer songwriter. One day New Orleans will flood.

One day came and it was time for me to stop wishing and start living...we'll begin in Belize.

Let's not forget why we are here

January 2007

Raining in Paradise

We have been back in San Pedro for a week, and I am less certain of where I am going, but more at ease with where I am.

The first few days were the beautiful San Pedro as we remembered it.

Our friend Alonzo is in a softball league and his team needed a pitcher. He was going to ask me to play until we played volleyball together and he saw what an utterly graceless athlete I am...these hands were made for strumming. Shelly, however, made an impression as she set up shots and moved around the court with the assurance she has in moments that require athletic skills. As the league is co-ed, she got the invite to join the team for a game. The field is in the center of town. Hard dirt with bottle caps, broken glass and stones everywhere, ensuring bad bounces. Most everyone played barefoot, ensuring bloody feet which seemed to bother no one but me. Half the folks in San Pedro had come out to play or to drink and watch their friends play. It is very like New Orleans in the neighborhood atmosphere, drinking at the ballpark and everyone knowing everyone. At first the guys on the team were wondering why Alonzo put this skinny American girl on the mound, but she pitched a good game, got a triple and won a spot on the roster for the season. The locals were surprised, and she was a star for the day. Some of the local high school team who were waiting to play the next game started to come by and give her high fives between innings. I just sat in the cheering section all day with a smile on my face watching Shelly be Shelly.

It has been raining for four days and I've written my second song in Spanish. The rain isn't non-stop, but good and strong, and everyday cloud bursts roll in from the Caribbean and soak the island. With dirt streets and bicycles for transportation, it makes for interesting days. You manage to stay dry if you keep your eyes open, but no way do you not get muddy.

I wonder about the folks coming to vacation for a few days and wish they could see it as we did on our first visit in all its sunshine and glory. I suppose if you only came on vacation for those four rain filled days you might be disappointed. But we are not here on vacation, we are here on retreat. Retreat from jobs, New Orleans, responsibility and choices.

For now we choose not to choose.

We have been so overwhelmed by sadness, uncertainty and choices for so long that we've given ourselves six months. Six months in paradise, six months of reflection, six months to let the natural ebb and flow of life lift us up and bring us back into the stream of existence. The greatest gift I've ever been given. Suspended in time in a beautiful and peaceful place.

Rain is another way to slow you down and take time to reflect.

It's raining in paradise but it's clear and sunny in our hearts. We are in love and in no hurry to go anywhere just yet.

Lost souls found in San Pedro

January 2007

Who Dat

The Saints are in the NFC Championship back home for the first time in their history, but Shell and I are in Belize. My friends want me to be excited for the team, but I'm not. I'm numb and don't care about football. I don't have a band anymore or a house, for that matter, most of my friends going crazy for the Saints don't have homes, but still they and the city have gone Who Dat crazy, and I'm glad because for a short while there is something to be happy about or at least some reason not to cry in New Orleans.

Who dat say 'dey gonna beat 'dem Saints? Give someone a Who Dat? this week. You don't have to be a Saints fan, you don't even have to be a football fan. You can simply be a fan of the indefatigable human spirit.

Who Dat? You can be a fan of hope in the face of despair. Who Dat? You can be a fan of choosing to live hand in hand with, and in the face of, absurdity. Who Dat? Who dat waiting for insurance money? Who dat waiting for Road Home help? Who dat rebuilding the city on their own with guts and hope for tomorrow? Who dat coming back in the face of government apathy and the most blatantly profiteering bunch of lame ducks and suckling ducklings in the history of America? Who dat say dey gonna beat dis city?

Keep New Orleans in your heart and give someone a Who Dat? this week. Folks in New Orleans deserve to be happy and have a party after a year and a half of daily uncertainty. For being pioneers in a modern age. For being.

Give someone a Who Dat this week.

On another note I saw Reggie Bush take a hit in the first quarter that reminded me why I like to watch football not play it. When I was a sophomore in high school at Redemptorist in the Irish Channel, I ill-advisedly went out for the football team with my best friend Mario. We were each 5' 3", weighed in at a strapping 125 lbs. And neither of us should have been there, which we quickly figured out. Mario and I managed to make one game, we had the cleanest uniforms and drank more Gatorade then anyone on the team. We decided to skip practice one day, drink cokes and hang out and loaf after school. We had a great time until the team bus rolled by and everyone spotted us. We stupidly decided to show up at practice the next day, and of course the coach did what coaches do in that situation. He had the team line up in single file and come at us one by one for us to take hits and get knocked down. I did fine for the first few hits, took them and waited for more. Then a guy hit me. Hit me so hard my arms and legs took a few seconds to catch up to my body. I picked up my arms and legs as I rolled end over end, landing on my feet it seems, because I don't remember standing up or looking back at the practice field. I walked through the St. Thomas Housing Projects, still wearing my uniform, all the way back to school and my guitar.

I guess in a way I owe that guy a big thank you because I've seen the world with my guitar, and all because he made me see stars. So wherever you are, thanks.

Who Dat?

January 2007

Paul Sanchez Solo Tour

I start my first solo tour post Cowboy Mouth in a few weeks and I'm excited about it.

It isn't actually my first solo tour. Back in '93, the Mouth had a few weeks off about the same time my first solo release, *Jet Black and Jealous*, came out. I booked a three week run up the East Coast so I could go play for my old buddies from my days living there playing in the anti-folk scene in New York City. The tour started at a club in Athens, Georgia, called Fred's. Even away from the Mouth that name seemed to dog me. At show time there was literally no one there. The owner apologized and mumbled something about the time being wrong in the ad but you know, things happen, and it was my first record so it was cool with me. No one knew who the Mouth was at the time, let alone little ol' Paul Sanchez. He said I should go downtown to a bar called The Globe and play on the street, that I could make some good money. I packed my acoustic and was walking to my car when four car loads of kids came pulling into the parking lot. One called out, "Where you going man, we came to see you?" I said, "Well I'm going down to play on the street in front of The Globe, come on down and you can see me for free."

We had a nice little caravan to downtown Athens and I set about playing, drew a nice crowd too. I noticed sitting inside the bar, looking through the glass at me and the scene on the corner was R.E.M.'s Michael Stipe. He couldn't hear me, he was on the inside. I'm sure it was a scene he'd witnessed countless times; he may have even busked on that same corner freshmen year for all I know. The moment wasn't special or striking. He didn't look in my eyes and silently recognize a song writing genius, I didn't get announced in Rolling Stone as his new favorite artist. He was just a guy having drinks with friends on a night off, and I was part of a scene on the sidewalk of his home town. Still, the symbolism of the moment struck me. Him on the inside looking out, me on the outside looking in. It's how it felt for me with the music business and would for many years. The Mouth got busy, solo work was not encouraged and I never did another extended solo tour in my time with the band.

I have loved sitting and strumming for folks since I was a kid, and for the first time in fifteen years I'll get to focus on singing my own songs. Playing them the way I feel and presenting myself to folks how I choose. I hope to walk, talk, sing and bring New Orleans to each show. Many of the shows are House Concerts which are private shows, but there are some dates at venues.

We had hoped to be in Belize another three months but the real world came crashing in on our dreams. The Mouth's business people are unwilling to discuss paying me any money of any kind, I had expected them to be tough but it was uglier than tough.

I had hugged Griff and Fred at the last Mouth show and told them I loved them. I'm glad I could leave while I still meant it because it would have been a drag to spend so much of my life with the band and leave in anger, it would have been stupid. I hugged them, though they did not hug back and would not speak to me. I e-mailed and phoned saying that it wasn't personal, that it was business, but they never got back to me, either of them. Griff sent a message through a friend that he wished me well but wasn't allowed to speak to me anymore. I still can't figure that one out. His parents are gone, he is divorced...who is there to ask permission from? I was cut off from my business and social network of the last decade and a half touring around the country.

It was as if I had never been a part of it, but I was growing to like that idea more and more.

While in Belize we also did the typical tourist thing and got swept away with island fever. In our grief we put down money on a condo in Belize hoping we could escape the pain of the past and live there forever. With money drying up back home, we tried to get out of the deal and get our down payment back. We had been told it would be no problem, but suddenly the fellow who swore it would be no problem said he had a boss to answer to and his boss was being unreasonable. We had trusted the guy we bought from because he was from Metairie, Louisiana, which is a suburb of New Orleans, and he really acted like he felt our loss back in New Orleans. Well you don't have to swim in the ocean or work in the music business to get bit by a shark and it's another lesson learned as we continue to get knocked around in life's flood waters.

I'm happy to move on with my life and music. Grateful to Kimball Packard for management help, and Chris Gerstner for having faith that folks out there would want to hear me sing and play. Kimball actually wanted me to stay in Cowboy Mouth for another year while he helped me set up a solo career, but I couldn't wait. It was time to move on, and as it turns out it has been very freeing musically and personally. I've started working with horn players, which is a gas having grown up in New Orleans, and look forward to playing some dates with a band this summer.

There are many different ways to play music, live life and love living and I mean to try several. That's what life is about, taking risks, feeling the thrill of the new and the hope of possibility. These shows represent new possibilities for me.

Celebrate that with me. New Possibilities. Yours and mine.

Mark 'Swag' Rosenzweig

February 2007

Lawrence and Beyond

"What's the life of a traveling troubadour like?"

I was asked that a couple of times at my first House Concert and it stumped me. Not just because I'm just getting started as a solo act, but because that, I suppose, is what I am now. I'd been doing House Concerts with Griff for a couple of years while on the road with the Mouth. We would show up at someone's house a couple of hours before a Mouth show in whatever town we happened to be playing, Griff and I would play our stuff for a couple of hours and then go back and play the Mouth show. It was fun and a way for us to play our own songs, but back then I was the guy in the rock band hopping off the tour bus to come sing for fans of the band. Now I'm an old time traveling troubadour, driving from town to town singing tunes and spinning tales. Cool for me. I've traveled playing music for the last sixteen years and it feels right to continue to do so.

How to explain it to the folks you love is something else. The friends who thought you'd be around for a po' boy again. The brother you miss and who misses you. You can't articulate for yourself what it is that makes you play, besides the act of playing, so you just go do it.

Tonight I'm in Kansas City. Last night was a House Concert in Lawrence. The hosts couldn't have been nicer or more respectful, and the guests were lovely. Listened, laughed, teared up and danced in all the right places.

Cool thing about House Concerts is that they are a success before you walk in the door. It's about the hosts and their friends as much as it is you. At venue shows you have to hope folks will leave the comfort of home, hearth and TIVO for a live experience which I admit, makes it sweet when folks do show up.

That's why I drove from New Orleans to here. To share some of my city as I remember it, my life as I've lived it and the songs that kept me breathing until love found me.

Playing a house party in Orlando with Susan Cowsill and Shamarr Allen.

February 2007

Down the Road

When I was in San Pedro, I would go down to the bar of El Pescador at cocktail hour to strum and sing for the guests waiting for dinner. There were folks from all over the world, and no one knew or cared that I had been in a rock band in America which was fine by me. They were happy to listen to me sing, and I found myself really digging the relaxed hang. Just strumming and singing whatever came into my head, or even better playing a request for someone making them and me happy. It was good to remember how the simple act of playing and singing to folks made me feel right.

In leaving the band I helped establish and played in for sixteen years, I took a leap of faith. A leap of faith in myself as a songwriter and story teller. Faith that folks might want to hear about my New Orleans in songs that were done a little differently than I'd been doing it. Sitting on a stool having some laughs with a few friends and singing all night long.

Always seemed like a good time to me and I had faith it would seem like a good time to other folks. I've done my first two venue shows, Kansas and St. Louis. Each club was in the black. People showed up, stayed and listened, laughed and danced along. I always knew the Midwest liked songwriters, now I know it in my heart. So my solo career is off to a fine beginning. Thanks for the support and shout outs that remind me to keep on moving down the road. I'm grateful for the chance to sit in a room full of people and feel a connection through songs.

March 2007

First Tour

Well what do you know? I played 17 shows in 21 days and except for missing Shelly so bad I couldn't breathe from time to time, wound up really digging it. For the most part, every show had people there who wanted to listen and that's all I wanted for the tour. That and to finish in the black, to go out, sing for folks and not lose money. Thanks to all of the House Concerts and the hosts who hired me. Thanks to the small venues that took a chance and booked me. Many thanks for listening to my stuff.

I don't have a master plan. One day at a time as I tiptoe towards a new life. Finished the tour in Nashville where several New Orleans friends who've moved here since the flood turned out for the show. Talk about folks who understand a fresh start. I sang about it, they felt it, are living their own fresh starts, and we're all hopeful that tomorrow holds a smile and the chance to replace the memories of pain and the flooded days with the possibilities of the now.

When I got home, I was going through some stuff and found the journal I used to keep when I was riding on the tour bus around the time the levees broke in New Orleans. It had this entry from Nashville the day after the flood:

"August 2005

In Nashville, mercifully on the road and embracing the life I helped create for fifteen years. I sat in an alley crying for New Orleans, its abandoned poor, the chaos and the innocent victims in its path. I noticed through my tears that I was sitting in a pattern of light, rectangles through the windows of an office building. The rectangles were surrounded by shadows, a chance pattern in the window of an interior design office. Following the pattern of light and shadows, my field of vision was lifted up from the alley, still following the pattern my eyes went past the sign For Ace Of Clubs which I played many times over the years now sitting shuttered and closed like New Orleans, like my home. The rectangles lead my eyes finally to the corner of the building then out to beautiful, pure sunlight and I remembered that light and love wait beyond these sad shadows."

March 2007

Home

Back in New Orleans and digging it.

Played the Station with Eddie Ecker on drums and Craig Klein on the trombone. What a gas. The kind of night I was hoping for when I decided to go my own way. Very New Orleans, a swinging good time, from the heart to the heart.

I'd always said if I couldn't make a living playing music I would work on movies again. I liked it better than anything I'd ever done for a living besides playing music. The money was good and I have a lot of friends still working in the business, so thought I might be able to get a favor from someone. Shelly landed a gig through an old friend of ours on the television show K-Ville when we got back. I called around trying to get movie work, but most of my friends were surprised to hear me looking for work, and almost everyone encouraged me to stick it out with music. I'm not sure if they are pulling for me that much, or if people know just how helpless I am with a tool belt on. I managed to land some second unit work on K-Ville for a few days. I ran into some folks I knew on the set or who knew me from the band. It seemed to make them a little uncomfortable that I was working a day job and not on a stage somewhere. No shame in bringing home a pay check. Aaron Neville worked on the docks to support his family between gigs. Lee Dorsey had a body and fender shop when he wasn't sitting in lal-la waiting for his ya-ya. A man does what he has to do to be the man he wants to be. I'm free to walk my own path, free to be home, free to be with my wife, free to be.

Playing tonight at d.b.a. on Frenchmen, the first of a few early shows I have lined up there in the coming weeks. I'll have space to find out who I am onstage, what I play, how I play it and say it. I like the room, the folks who work there and am grateful for the gigs.

I love being in New Orleans. Home.

April 2007

Sitting In

Been sitting in on some John Boutté gigs.

What a different and beautiful world jazz is. In every way, it's the opposite approach to music than rock and roll. John's drummer, Herman Le Beau is going on tour with Elvis Costello this summer, and he asked me what I could tell him about playing rock and roll as compared to jazz. I told him to play like he did when he first learned how to play and was afraid of being found out. Loud, hard and desperate. I told him what I tell jazz guys who ask me about playing rock. I told him if he felt the urge to play a fill during a song that he should fight it with every fiber of his being, that when he couldn't stand it anymore to play the fill one time and never again.

The guys in John's band are very cool to me. They take time to teach me a little about their music whenever we play together. They teach without telling, won't answer if asked because I don't know how to ask it and wouldn't understand it if they explained it to me. So we play, I learn by sticking out when I don't want to, by listening and learning to blend in. It's fun, as well as an honor, to play with guys who have invested this much time into playing their instrument for the sake of the music. Not for getting press, bright lights, tour buses or promises of fame and fortune.

Makes me glad to be home.

I'll be playing with them at French Quarter Fest next week and it is a joy to hear musicians of that caliber play my stuff. Last week at my Sunday d.b.a. show David Torkanowsy sat in on piano and accordion and took my breath away with what he brought to my stuff. Mark Mullins, Craig Klein and Matt Perrine will be backing me at the Concert in the Square series on the Wednesday between Jazz Fest weekends. Then there's the Carrollton Station gig with my friends from Beatin' Path who will insist I rock again with the force of their onstage energy.

That's a good few weeks in New Orleans for me.

John Boutté and me enjoying the French Quarter

April 2007

Jazz Fest

This is the first Jazz Fest in sixteen years that I won't be playing on the Fair Grounds and I have to admit, I'll miss it. It was one of the coolest gigs ever for me because I started going to Fest when I was fifteen, working in a beer booth. I would 'accidentally' puncture a can while chopping ice and, "oops, have to drink that one." I saw Odetta, Pete Seeger, Johnny Adams. I learned about music that wasn't on WTIX, the a.m. radio station I grew up with in New Orleans.

When I started playing gigs there it was like a dream come true.

It was a neighborhood experience and I used to ride my bike to the gig. I didn't plan on leaving the Mouth and did so on the spur of the moment, and the Fest was already booked.

Maybe next year. Either way I'll always be grateful to Quint Davis for letting me play there at all. This year I get to be a fan, and what a year to be a fan. The first weekend weather was picture perfect. Blue skies, warm enough to keep you sucking down brews but not so hot that you wanted to split. The Trout Baquet from Li'l Dizzy's. Let me say it again, the Trout Baquet, Dear Lord. I went back twice. Kicked off the whole experience with Tambourine Lady in the Gospel Tent. Feeling sanctified and uplifted, I set about a weekend so long, fun and rich with music that I struggle to recall.

Trombone Shorty making me smile remembering what that kind of youthful passion is like and making me proud to be from New Orleans. So much good music I had to limit myself to four songs an act on Saturday so I could see it all.

The Bone Loop: T-Bone Burnett, Bonerama and Trombone Shorty all playing at the same time. It was exhausting and exhilarating, and I saw them all.

On Sunday I parked at the Gentilly Stage for Theresa Andersen, New Orleans Social Club (who should be closing a stage they were so brilliantly, authentically, New Orleans), Miss Irma Thomas, the Soul Queen of New Orleans and Bonnie Raitt closing the stage. Bonnie was brilliant, understands New Orleans, gets what Jazz Fest is about and gave the people love which they gave right back.

That's just the daytime stuff.

The nighttime is full of memories of Frenchmen Street, Boutté singing, Trombone Shorty's band blowing the roof off Cafe Brazil, too many glasses of La Crema at d.b.a, Big Sam and the Funky Nation at Brazil.

It's Monday, I'm exhausted and my weekend of being a fan is over. Tomorrow I start working with Boutté for the Threadhead Benefit, next day in the Square and the weekend at the Station.

Man it's great to be home for Fest.

Young man leading a second line at Jazz Fest

May 2007

Beyond Fest

I made it through another Jazz Fest. Survived is the correct word. How much music, fun, food, alcohol, laughs, dancing and living can you squeeze into two weekends? Come to Jazz Fest and find out what you're made of.

Made a new friend during Fest, a fellow named Colman deKay from L.A. He is a screenwriter. My old friend Vance DeGeneres called and asked me to say hello to some folks that were in town for Fest. Colman was staying a couple of blocks down on Royal Street and we kept bumping into each other on the street. We would wind up hanging out a lot and found we really dug each other's company. I found out that Colman is friends with, and occasionally works with, the film director Steven Soderbergh. I had known Steven briefly when we were young. In fact, keeping the world small, Steven had directed a video for a band I had in the eighties called The Backbeats. Vance was in the band as was the Mouth's second bass player, Steve Walters, and Fred on drums. We were a minor local hit. Steven was a young student at L.S.U. at the time and liked the band enough to offer to shoot a video of us. The video was shot in black and white and was, naturally, quite good. Ahead of its time, better than most videos on MTV and not because we were any great shakes as a band, but because even in this early bit of work, with no budget and little talent in front of the cameras, Steven Soderbergh showed a glimpse of what he would become as a director. The band broke up just before he finished the editing, and we never paid him for the video so he kept it which we all agreed was fair enough. I believe our not paying him was the final straw in getting him fired from the small editing house in Baton Rouge where he was working at the time. Still he remembered us later on and used the Mouth in a scene for one of his later films, The Underneath.

Steven was coming to town to screen a film and give a talk on it at the Canal Place Cinema, and Colman called him and got us invited. It was good to see Steven, good to know that he remembered me after all these years. After he gave his talk a few of us went for a drink nearby while his film was running. As luck (bad luck) would have it, the bartender was a fan of my old band. He was "hooking me up" by serving me double white russians which taste like candy and go down even faster, on the house. After the screening, several of us went back with Steven to the hotel where he was staying for some wine and talk of going to Frenchmen Street came up. I was glad because I was starting to feel like I needed a little air. I had already unleashed a little, slightly drunk, Katrina anger at the government, which wasn't well received, and I wanted to clear my head so I could enjoy the company of someone I had known in my youth. It is quite something to stand next to the people you dreamed with in your youth when you know their dreams have become reality, it makes one feel like anything is possible. Steven was excited about his new film, "The Good German", and wanted to screen it for Colman and his film buddies. While I was hoping for Frenchmen Street, fresh air and music, I was content to settle in and watch the film. Unfortunately for me, double white russians and red wine don't mix. The film had not been scored yet and editing was ongoing. It is a film noir piece, black and white, dark and mysterious. The room was closing in; I was getting a little dizzy and knew I had to get out of there even if it meant leaving in the middle of the film. On all fours, I scooped up my shoes, mumbled an excuse about my wife waiting up for me and split before I had the chance to pass out. I was so mortified the next day that I didn't call Colman until seven at night to ask how the evening went and apologize for getting Katrina-sad-drunk and cutting out so abruptly. When I said I was sorry for leaving early Colman said, "You were there? Man, I was so drunk I didn't even remember you had come with me." Which true or not, made me feel better and cemented a growing friendship, as the last thing a New Orleanian wants is grief about getting drunk, especially post-K. He also told me that he had gotten mugged walking back home that night so our time of innocent emptiness has ended as well.

By Tuesday morning after the Fest, my throat hurt from all the singing and shows I played at the Station and Lafayette Square. With Ecker driving, I slept all the way to Atlanta for a show there. I was as beat as an old plough mule, but my soul was shining like a diamond.

My favorite comment, and the one I hear from friends, fans and family, is how happy Shelly and I look. Folks can see a sparkle in our eyes and a skip in our steps. Our life belongs to us again and it feels wonderful. I've never been happier or more fulfilled professionally than these last three months. Like I've picked up a thread laid aside for too long.

I'm at peace with my choice to follow that new path to the waterfall.

Do I stumble?
Yes.

Do I feel uncertain?
Sometimes.

This is my path now and I'll walk it. Comfortable in my own skin for the first time in over a decade.

If you are considering a change in your life and have fears and uncertainties, then I urge you to make the leap.

The leap of faith, of hope, of promise.

Life is going by whether you make the change or not. Will you feel better in ten years having tried to live your dream or remembering that you once had one?

June 2007

Chi-Town is My Town

Chicago I love ya'.

Paul Sanchez and The Rolling Road Show played a gig at HOB in Chicago. It was a truly wonderful evening for us all. I had my friends from Beatin' Path in the band on this one. Eddie Ecker on drums and jokes, Skeet Hanks and his amazing voice, and my old friend Mike Mayeux playing lead guitar. David Torkanowsky, who has been a musical guide since I got back to town-from telling me how to pick a band to telling me how to go about making it a business-flew himself up for the gig just to help me out, and was his usual mad genius, brilliant self.

I arrived late and a bit frazzled from the journey but as soon as I entered the room I got so much love that I had to catch my breath and soak in all that beautiful energy. Folks giving me hugs, showing up with open hearts to help me continue to be me. People from Chicago, folks who drove in from St. Louis, Ohio, flew in from New Orleans.

Sonia and I were buzzing the whole sixteen hour drive back to New Orleans. We felt refreshed and blessed, like we were really making music from the heart and enjoyed a real exchange of energy with the folks in the room.

Paris Delane, a singer from Chicago with a gorgeous baritone voice, got on stage for 'You Are My Sunshine' and everyone on stage was singing like a New Orleans brass band of voices riffing off each other, swinging with the moment. Paris lifted the crowd with the power of his voice and spirit and I felt like I was in the Gospel Tent at Jazz Fest.

From the moment we arrived, the HOB production staff treated us with the same love and respect as they have for the last decade. It was nice because for years the band I was in had sold out the big room but I was there to play the small room yet the respect from the staff was the same. It felt like it always does, like home.

What a night.

We played like children, with smiles on our faces and joy in our very being as if playing were the most fun thing we could ever do, which of course it is supposed to be.

Sonia sang some of my songs, 'Mexico' and 'Lonely Wasted and Blue' as well as some of her own. Skeet did 'Light It On Fire' and 'Louisiana Lowdown and Blue'. Eddie sang 'All Alone'. Paris sang again on 'Lil' Liza Jane/Iko' and 'Foot of Canal Street' and the whole audience sang along like they were part of the band.

A night I've waited for and will treasure.

I finally let go of my life raft and am floating with the current, as Richard Bach once wrote, getting a little smashed on the rocks as I rise to the surface to float, to fly where the universe decides.

With Sonia and Eddie in Chicago

June 2007

Camp Summer Tribe

Leaving tomorrow for a tour.

Starting over has been every bit as fulfilling as I'd hoped it would be, even though it has been a little more difficult then I'd anticipated. I thought there would be some financial help from my past, but I am on my own so it's up to me to keep moving forward. If the longest journey begins with a single step, then how long is the journey that is one step up, two steps back. Sometimes I get tired, as I'm sure you do with your job, your life, your attempts to be a good person and still try to glimpse a dream.

Played in Ohio last weekend with John Boutté and his band. What a joy to share space with such wonderful musicians. Shannon Powell, New Orleans jazz drumming legend, is one of the funniest people ever and a great New Orleans cook. After we played a cocktail hour set, our host told us to go relax for a little while and that he would be taking us out for a steak dinner in a couple of hours. I was walking back to the house where the musicians were staying on this beautiful lake in Ohio with Shannon and Boutté's bass player, Peter Harris, when Shannon rubbed his stomach and said, "U-u-u-m, steak dinner sounds good. I wonder if I can get that driver to give me a lift to the store so I can get a little snack before dinner." Peter and I continued to the house to get some sleep because we were playing another set after dinner and Shannon went off to find the driver our host had hired for the weekend.

I woke up some time later or I might say was grabbed awake by my nostrils smelling the most delicious cooking you could ever want to wake to. Downstairs in the kitchen, Shannon was at the stove with a towel draped over his shoulder, a stirring spoon in one hand and a half-eaten pork chop in the other. He explained that he didn't want to go to dinner hungry so he had made a little something. As Peter came into the kitchen rubbing his sleepy head and sniffing the air, Shannon fixed him a plate saying he should eat a little something so he didn't show up for dinner too hungry. Man, there was no way the restaurant was going to top this. He had made smothered pork chops, mac and cheese, string beans and potatoes. It was no snack, it was a meal and a delicious one. While I was debating whether it was a good idea to eat right before dinner, a woman from the house across the street knocked on the door. A very nice, and as we were staying in a resort type place, very wealthy lady. She smiled and said she had smelled the cooking from her house and would it be possible to taste it. Shannon being the larger than life, New Orleans-crazy-but-sweet kind of cat that he is fixed her a plate to take home. She was very excited and headed back home with a little skip in her step. A few moments later she knocked again and asked if she could have a plate for her husband because the food was so good she didn't want to share and her husband wouldn't stop asking. Shannon laughed and began fixing another to-go plate at which point my debate ended and I chowed mightily not caring what might happen at dinner. As it turns out dinner was terrific but it didn't touch the cooking of Shannon Powell when he wanted to "throw a little snack together."

The music was sublime (John's band is great), and the folks putting us up for the weekend were most generous. Came home exhausted and getting ready to hit the road again. It all felt too fast, I had too little time with Shell before leaving again, too much to do, such a mountain I've decided to climb.

During the trip home I was more tired then I remembered being on short trips and I seemed to be feeling over-heated a bit. I tried to ignore it and push through. When I got home from the airport Shelly was at work. I had a bite, a shower and started laundry. I remember walking through the bedroom and then I woke up on the floor. I felt like I did that day in Chicago when I got hit by the taxi. I was over-heated and had to throw up. I laid on the couch and slept for the rest of the day. By the time Shelly got home, I had recovered and didn't tell her about it. We are doing our best to remake our lives, there is so much work to do, I don't have time to be sick, I can't be sick, I won't be sick.

I'd almost forgotten that I'd promised the folks from Camp Summer Tribe that I would sing for them. I've sung for them every August for the last decade or so. Camp Summer Tribe takes children with Cerebral Palsy and Downs Syndrome to Fontainebleau State Park on the north shore of Lake Ponchatrain for two weeks during the summer. The intent is to give the kids a summer camp experience, to give their parents a little break from the twenty-four hour a day job it is to care for the children and hopefully relieve a little pressure for all involved. The camp is run by adult volunteers and each child is assigned a high school student as an attendant. The students volunteer initially for extra credit but over the years I've seen the high school kids changed by their experience and many come back year after year, some have gone on to become the adult chaperones at the camp. I play for them every year and had promised to do so again this year. I was pressed for time in so many ways and didn't think I could pull it off, or if I had it in me to leave Shelly for the night to make the thirty mile drive across the lake and back when I was taking off the next morning for a long tour. Then I went and played for them. Played for kids who suffer greater challenges just to wake up and exist than I've ever known. Kids with little control over their bodies but with the ability to smile and sing and feel alive through the music I played them and the energy they let the songs create. Their high school attendants were so beautiful, so committed to laughter with these kids for those few days. It's really what makes the camp so hopeful and full of promise because they are the living example of both.

I've played for this group every summer for the last ten years and it teaches me the same lessons every time, gratitude and humility.

When I think my life is hard or my challenge to be is too great, I remember the kids of Camp Summer Tribe who embrace challenge as their life. I think of the people doing more to help others than themselves for that week. Sleeping in tents and caring for kids who can't care for themselves, making it so much fun for the children, so unforgettable for anyone who witnesses it.

I'm so blessed to have spent so many years doing something I love, to have love in my life. To be exactly where I am facing the challenges of today with love in my heart and hope for the future.

August 2007

Perspective

I wanted to write about how much I miss Shelly now that she works in New Orleans and I travel on my own.

I wanted to write about how uncertain life feels.

I wanted to write about the new record I'll be making at the end of the summer.

I called Dave Pirner, who had taken his family to Minneapolis for the summer, to discuss some ideas I had for the upcoming recording sessions. Dave had taken his family to his hometown of Minneapolis to get away from hurricane season and Katrina memories. The day I called was the day after the bridge collapse had caused panic and sadness to grip their city, a bridge over the Mississippi River ironically enough. I had called to talk about the record not even realizing where they were and not thinking how they might have been affected by this terrible thing. Before I had a chance to ask about the record, he started talking right away about how everyone was safe, that I needn't worry about them and how it was like Katrina flash backs with the helicopters and the patchy phone service, the air of despair and confusion around the city.

While he was talking, I realized that for me it was a sad news story I read before I started my day. I didn't give it much thought beyond remembering how many times over the years of touring I'd been on that bridge and might not have mentioned it in our conversation if he hadn't reminded me.

I thought back over the last couple of years since the flood at my anger, sadness and confusion as I watched people around the country care less and less about New Orleans and I understood.

Folks do care, but life keeps throwing things at you and maybe you have to keep some defense up. Maybe you have to remember to care.

I don't know, I have no answers or explanations. I know the folks up there and the folks down here will be digging out long after the bridges, levees and houses have been rebuilt.

I love my wife.

I keep trying to play music to more and more folks.

Life is going by and I'm just trying to dig it.

Living in New Orleans

August 2007

Fun with Friends

I'm looking forward to hitting the road with Mary, Sonia and Eddie.

What a joy to travel and play with people you dig. Got a smile on my face thinking about it. I only wish Shelly could come because she would enjoy the company as much or more than me.

I love Shelly for giving me space to do what I do even as it takes me away from her and gives us both a sadness we won't admit to. She reminds me every day to enjoy the moment, whatever it brings. She recently surprised me with a cell phone free weekend at a French Quarter hotel. Sitting on the roof top having a glass of wine at sunset I remembered that our adventure together was the best part of the last several years of the band. I never would have stayed in as long as I did if she hadn't been there to share it.

I travel without her now, which is hard, but I like the music I'm playing a lot more. The truth is Shelly and I both get treated much better by the people we work with and for, so we are happier.

Our adventure continues because we want it to.

Our adventure is something we invented, something we live in our love.

So I'm hitting the road with friends.

Friends making music.

Healing.

August 2007

Two Years Ago

Two years ago today my wife and I had a house that was paid for completely.

Shelly's grandfather built the house, her mom grew up there, met her dad there. She used to make him hop the fence in the driveway for kisses.

We had just spent thirty thousand dollars renovating.

My wife did most of the work while I was in the studio making music. She dealt with the contractors, which confused them to no end the times I was there as I sat with a blank stare having no idea what they were talking about. She did the demolition herself to save money and got her friend Christy to come by and help her drag out the heavy stuff. Chose everything from paint colors to what kind of roof we would have.

In an interview after the flood she was asked what achievement in her life she was most proud of and her answer was renovating her own home.

Two years ago I was in a band that I'd spent sixteen years with, guys I considered family.

Two years ago I had a community of friends, shared experiences, places to eat, drink, meet and laugh. Phones rang and the playgrounds were full of kids, traffic lights functioned, people worked, went to school, lived, grumbled and loved as they had done for generations.

Now everyday is the unexpected.

We live with a desperate eye for any sign of hope, but we live with an ambivalence about living that we struggle to control and deny.

We dance, but still yearn for the feeling of freedom dancing once gave.

We listen, no, we hang on every note of music like it is water in the desert, which is what it has become.

It has never sounded sweeter to hear the music that's been around us all our lives.

The sweet sounds reminding us of what was, is, and will always be a part of us.

I read a story recently on mental health which said there is no measuring stick for recovery because we aren't having flashbacks or post traumatic stress, we live in ruins every day.

Those who live in Lakeview, Gentilly, the Lower Nine, in the neighborhoods where being back means accepting that you may live in the only inhabited house on the block.

This past Sunday it was overcast and the first cool breezes since early summer were blowing.

The place we live in now is in a neighborhood that was flooded. It's small, has only two windows and no porch.

We wanted to be out in the cool breeze but Shelly works long hours on the television show K-Ville and really wanted to not leave home.

The solution was a funny/sad irony of life here in the real K-Ville. We sat on the porch of the house next door.

Gutted and empty there was no one to mind as we sat out and smelled the rain and the Ponchatrain, watching the lightning show.

Having a glass of wine and doing what we have all learned to do here in the last two years, accept that this is our life, make the most of our time together and enjoy what is.

Thanks to everyone around the country who gave and are giving support in the ways that you do, even if it's just listening.

September 2007

Three Cheers for September

September is here.

Labor Day and the dog days of summer behind us, hooray!

I don't care what T.S. Elliot says, August is the cruelest month of the year in New Orleans. With its memories of floods, its oppressive heat, humidity so thick you can almost breathe liquid air and, worst of all, the malaise. No one wants to do anything and, try as we might, even hanging out with your best buddies doesn't sound as good as a nap in an air conditioned place or even a cool breeze blowing anywhere on or near you.

The first day of September I went out for my morning run, the air was cooler, the sunrise prettier.

We can venture out without fear of drowning in our own sweat or in our neighborhoods for that matter. We can socialize without dripping on each other which is nice. The feeling of 'party' that is life in New Orleans most of the year is in the air.

The party that kicks off with Saints season, blazes through Voodoo Fest and into Thanksgiving. Now we're really cooking as we party through the New Year like everyone else, but New Year's Eve is really just a tune up party for Mardi Gras, St. Patrick's Day Parades, to keep us in shape for French Quarter Fest and Jazz Fest (possibly the best party anywhere) when the pace, mercifully, begins to slow down to prepare us for the oppressive hibernation of August.

I told some folks from L.A. who are in town working on K-Ville that they would get ribbons for making it through August. Now I have to explain that the ribbon is the glow from the first of many evenings out enjoying the city.

September 2007

Positive Energy, Hard Work and Moving On

I've written a lot about loss and acceptance, but life has a way of moving on when you're not looking.

Today I am digging what I have in my life and enjoying what is. My wife likes her job and loves me. That seems a fine start to a good life for me.

I waited my whole life to get around to playing my songs for folks and it's been wonderful. In the last nine months I've played over a hundred shows around the country on my own and with other folks.

Had the chance to sing on my first jazz record, Shamarr Allen's *Meet Me On Frenchmen Street*, where I sang the song 'Do You Know What It Means To Miss New Orleans'.

Sang back up on a country record with Susan Cowsill, and I recorded 'If I Only Had A Brain' with Shamarr for a children's record featuring other New Orleans artists called *Funky Kidz*.

I've played with some of the finest musicians in the city of New Orleans, and had the pleasure of hearing my music grow and become richer through the sounds of their horns, pianos, voices and drums.

I run in the mornings, spend my days keeping Paul Sanchez Music business in order; thank goodness the computer and QuickBooks do most of the work. In the evenings when I'm not working I go out to see the musicians who lift my soul and make me glad to be from New Orleans. I have a long way to go before there is steady income and steady work but Shelly is supportive and I believe in positive energy, hard work and moving on.

I have been looking for a connection to something for a long time and I found it right here where I started.

The music, the people, the feeling that life is for living and work shouldn't be taken too seriously.

The sense of community in the streets, talking to people you know and people you don't with the same familiarity.

The magic hasn't been lost and that was, I guess, what we all feared the most as events of the Thing unfolded. Ultimately the magic is in each of us anyway.

The moment that feels like sublime perfection when a John Boutté sings or a Shamarr Allen plays his horn on a night when you know the rest of the country is tucked in, is only wonderful if you open up and allow yourself to experience it.

Shelly and me riding our bikes through the Quarter

September 2007

Not Really a Mystery

I'm so honored, humbled and excited to work with the musicians we've assembled for *Exit to Mystery Street*.

Dave Pirner, lead singer of Soul Asylum producing, Ivan Neville on B3, Raymond Weber of Dumpstaphunk on drums, Matt Perrine on bass and tuba, David Torkanowsky on piano and accordion, James Andrews and Shamarr Allen on trumpet, Craig Klein of Bonerama and Big Sam of Big Sam's Funky Nation on trombones, Fredy Omar joining me to sing two songs in Spanish, Sonia Tetlow on guitar and mandolin, and Susan Cowsill on vocals.

If you're a fan of New Orleans music you can probably understand my excitement at working with the names I've just listed. Honestly it would be a joy if I was recording with them for someone else's material and the fact that it's mine has me over the moon with anticipation.

It's also exciting to make a real New Orleans record.

I grew up in the Irish Channel in New Orleans with five brothers and five sisters which means I experienced New Orleans music from every decade. I learned to slow dance to Art Neville's 'All These Things' and Aaron's 'Wrong Number, I'm Sorry, Good-bye'. I was on my way to a seventh grade party and didn't know how to dance. My sister Margie gave me a lesson to those songs.

I danced that night and have been dancing ever since.

I've searched my whole life for a feeling that feels like belonging, and I believe I've found it.

I never felt quite at home in the folk world (too loud and drunk) or the rock world (not loud or drunk enough, though I certainly did my best), and I had always tried to approach each separately.

This approach feels like the marriage of what I love about both music worlds, and really it's just New Orleans. It's the sound of the river, the Quarter, the Marigny, the Channel. The sound of tomorrow and the sound of yesterday. It is the sound of home and the feeling of belonging.

I hope to represent the music of my city with passion and honesty and couldn't be happier to be sharing that experience with so many musicians whose work I admire.

I only wish I had twice the budget so I could include more of New Orleans' talented players.

Stephen Walker and Shamarr Allen and me... doing what we do!

October 2007

Recording Exit to Mystery Street

I began recording my new release *Exit to Mystery Street* yesterday.

A fantastic day and a fantastic band. These guys were simply smoking.

Raymond Weber is bad on so many levels I need a step ladder to stand with him. Matt Perrine is incredibly fun to work with. He and Raymond locked in on concepts and aesthetics, and songs jumped to life in front of me. Matt played electric bass, stand up acoustic bass and tuba; he was surrounded in the bass world and happy to be there and both of them playing any groove I threw at them. Of course my right hand man Sonia was playing mandolin and electric guitar as steady and inspired as both the very serious players she was playing with. Me, I was happy as a kid in a candy store.

My songs were in the hands of people who were taking them places so beautiful that I was thrilled and humbled. Dave Pirner was producing, rearranging songs, creating energies on songs and keeping a hand on where the session was technically and musically. Guiding the music and also letting the music guide him when we slide down a New Orleans path that is unfamiliar to him. He steps back and lets the great players we've hired show him where this roast beef gravy dripping groove is going.

I've seen it in my head and heard this record playing louder and louder in my ears for months now. Now it's real and it's an exhilarating experience to lose myself in.

Exit to Mystery Street is swinging and I'm digging the process as much as I'll dig getting it out to y'all.

On stage with Sonia

October 2007

A Great Two Weeks

Just coming up for air after the most enjoyable two weeks of my professional career.

I went in to Truck Farm Studios for twelve straight days to record my new release, *Exit to Mystery Street*, with Dave Pirner producing; also to record a new disc with John Boutté, songs he and I have written which will also be produced by Dave called *Good Neighbor*.

After booking the session I got an offer from the YLC in New Orleans to do a Wednesday at the Square concert, Paul Sanchez and the Rolling Road Show with special guest, Ivan Neville sitting in. It was too interesting to pass up even though I already had the two studio sessions to tend to...a little bit exhausting and a little bit of heaven.

Raymond Weber is the most creative, fun and steady drummer I've ever had the pleasure to record with, and every basic track begins with the sound of Raymond laughing and many of them end with that lovely sound.

When we did the first take of the first track, which was 'Door Poppin', Pirner turned to the engineer, George, and said, "Turn off the click track, it's an insult to a drummer this good."

Matt Perrine on bass, stand up bass and tuba was a melodic, thumping spark of inspiration and my first experience playing with a tuba which is all I want on bass now. I honestly think there is no groove he can't play and turn into its own melody within the song.

Sonia, who has been my steady friend and riding partner for these past several months, came up with great parts on both lead guitar and mandolin and was as happy as could be to play music with all the great musicians coming through the session.

Pirner thought it all a bit crazy and on the verge of out of control, and occasionally he would pull his bucket hat over his eyes and wait for the madness to end or turn into music. I also think he got a kick out of being smack dab in the middle of the flow of New Orleans music and musicians that week.

We made up horn ideas as we went along, but when it's James Andrews, Big Sam, Craig Klein and Shamarr on horns you know where it's headed before the train leaves the station. With a line up like that you are headed to a second line, a good time, you're headed to Gloryland.

Ivan Neville on the B3 was something I won't forget. He came in to record B3 on 'Door Poppin'' which he hadn't heard before. I asked if he wanted to hear the tune first and he said no. I explained that he would be playing a solo and didn't he want to at least hear the original song he'd never even heard before let alone played, "you know, to hear the structure." He indulged me for a moment and said sure let's hear it for structure, we listened to one verse and chorus then he said "Turn it off and let's play, I don't want to spoil it." It's all instinct, heart and soul when he plays and it's a pretty amazing sight.

Alex McMurray came in for a lead guitar track and transformed something that was just wood and wire into a live fire-breathing dragon of which he was master. It was scary to watch and mind blowing to know that all that bad ass playing was on one of my tunes. He lives next door to Truck Farm and we were working on the song 'Ride With the Devil'. Originally we weren't going to have that song on the record, it wasn't on the list, but Ivan was rockin' the room the day he came in to track. Matt and Raymond were there and Dave decided to record it. He came up to me with that Midwestern drawl he hasn't lost in a decade plus of living among us Y'ats and said, "Hey ma-a-a-n, Ivan is really ri-i-i-pping. What do you say we record 'Ride With the Devil'?" I said, "You know Dave, I spent a lot of years playing rock and I got burned by my old band. I just don't think I want any rock songs on this record." He smiled, tugged at his bucket hat and said, "Well ma-a-a-n, that's cool and all but a lot of folks still like rock n' roll and we're going to put some on this record." After we had tracked it and Ivan split, we were taking a break in the back yard when Dave said what the song really needed was some ripping lead guitar. I told him that wasn't me, I don't rip, rock guitar. I said we'd have to find someone. He turned and pointed to the yard next door and said, "He can." I'd never met Alex McMurray but had heard about him and his amazing song writing for years. At this particular moment he was working in his garden, sweaty, his face was dirty and his arms had taken the worst of a battle with poison ivy in the yard he was trying to clear. Dave asked if he felt like rockin' and he said sure. He went next door and got his guitar and walked in to the studio, still dirty and with lotion on his arms for the poison ivy, plugged in and there was the dragon. My jaw dropped as he laid down some nasty, nasty guitar, just a few takes. Dave thanked him after the third or fourth pass. He kind of blinked, unplugged and said, "Thanks man, I don't get to play that kind of guitar too often in New Orleans," and went back to his gardening.

We recorded 'Adios San Pedro', which was my good-bye to the people of Belize who took Shelly and me in after the flood and gave us a place to rest and heal. Freddie Omar, the Salsa King of Frenchmen Street, sang a duet with me on the track. Freddie is from Honduras originally, not far from San Pedro. The beautiful lilt in his tenor reminded me of the easy way of island life, the more intense baritone of my voice reminding me that I have returned and survived.

Susan Cowsill and the orchestra of voices within her brought the right touch of June to my Johnny on 'Johnny and His June', which I wrote with Mary Lasseigne and Shelly, a track meant to honor outlaw love. Susan's layered harmonies make 'Sedation' sound like a cross between the Beatles, Beach Boys and XTC. She sang about five harmonies on the song and heard another twenty in her head that she could have sung.

The budget was tight. Dave and the engineer, George Ortolano, worked nose to the grindstone until collapsing from hunger and exhaustion. Those two guys never let up, and we hustled players through the studio with far less time to socialize than I would have liked, but we got amazing stuff from so many people. All of it added to the sound of New Orleans the record is becoming, the sounds I grew up with and carry around in my head and heart.

With no days off we headed straight into John Boutté's session.

It is something I've wanted to do for a long time. To record a disc of songs with John that we wrote together. To tell his fascinating story, the story of the Tremé and jazz. The story and history of New Orleans sung by one of the most beautiful voices I ever heard. John had decided to include Dave in this record as well and I feel very fortunate that fate placed both projects in Dave's hands. While we both mystified him occasionally with our language, rhythms and ways, he embraced much of it, endured all of it, and developed a vision of my songs and John's songs that went further than anything I had planned or could have imagined. We both trusted him and followed him to some interesting places musically.

In the middle of John's sessions I had to leave early one day for the gig in the Square with Ivan.

I'd been so focused on the studio that we only had time to trade e-mails and write a set of songs we both figured we'd know. At sound check that evening it was an effortless flow as we traded vocals on 'You Don't Know Me' by Ray Charles. It was like we'd sung together all our lives. The band was great. Ivan is so soulful, Big Sam got on stage and played a few with us and we threw in a song he sings, 'Rock Me Baby/Whole Lotta Shaking' and he stomped the stage 'til it shot sparks of fun over the crowd. It was the most exciting, musical and fun concert I ever got to be part of in my life and something I'll remember for a long time. Music how it was meant to be, real sharing, real joy and real energy sweeping out over the audience who gave it right back.

That night I passed out at home. Shelly was there this time and there was no hiding it. She heard a crash in the bathroom, found me slumped over the tub with water running on my face and I wasn't coming to. Poor Shell was so scared all she could do was pull me out of the tub and hold me until I woke up. Then she put me to bed and called a doctor friend for advice. I'm supposed to go see someone, but I think I've just been working too hard but she is scared so I may have to get checked out.

The next morning I was back at work on John's record and got to sit for a day and listen to that wonderful voice deliver eight hours of lead vocal performances until he was too sweaty and exhausted to continue. It was a heroic performance and Dave was impressed at Boutté's stamina and his resolve to finish the project. He watched as John worked to exhaustion and was ready to work some more if needed. Dave finally walked out to the studio, gave him a hug, told him he was great, to go home.

We all gave every bit of energy, love and music to these two projects and I hope y'all dig them when you hear them.

I have never been so satisfied with an experience and resulting recording than I am with both of these. Thanks very much to Chris and Jill Gertsner from St. Louis for helping to make *Exit to Mystery Street* possible, and thanks to Chris Joseph and the Threadheads for giving John and me a chance to document our friendship, mutual respect and songs on John's record, *Good Neighbor*.

Playing a Road Show with Ivan Neville

John Boutté

October 2007

It's All About the Music

My Lafayette Square show was such a sweet night for me that I wanted to share more of it.

The song 'Home' which was written in the days after the flood was sung by Craig Klein from Bonerama and Shamarr Allen. Craig lost his home in St. Bernard Parish and he sings the first verse, "It's hard in St. Bernard, there's tears in Algiers, if you're calling for New Orleans there's nobody here." Shamarr Allen lost his home near the levee breach in the Ninth Ward and sings the next verse, "The Ninth Ward's disappeared, the Tremé's overflowed."

Big Sam of Big Sam's Funky Nation was playing trombone and he had only recently moved back to New Orleans. Ivan, Mary, me, all of our lives changed by this thing and the song seemed to have more depth than it ever had before.

'The Foot of Canal Street' was a swinging New Orleans good time with the whole band taking solos, including percussionist Herbert Stevens playing a second line tambourine solo.

Exit to Mystery Street is in the mixing phase, and while this phase feels slowest of all I can also hear the record coming into focus and I'm digging it. It's what I wanted and then some.

The Boutté record, *Good Neighbor*, is coming along beautifully as well. I got the rough mixes yesterday and it is a lovely and earthy record. While I only sing one or two songs on the record (the Threadheads had originally wanted a duo record), John and I wrote most of them and made this record together. It feels like a representation of our friendship as well as a recording of music.

It is so fulfilling to get this much music in the world that I can endorse completely and happily.

Hope you dig it whenever you hear it.

Craig Klein

November 2007

Happy Birthday/Independence to Me

A year ago I played my last show as a founding member of Cowboy Mouth.

I'd played with them for sixteen years. Met my wife with them. Buried my mother and the brother who taught me to play guitar. Lost my city, my home and my way as a Cowboy.

I also had a lot of fun and adventure traveling around the world with the band because my wife was with me for fourteen of those years and we tried to take advantage of the experiences life offered.

I quit for many reasons and knew that I had an uphill battle to start over from scratch. I thought folks would know about my songs from my years in the Mouth, but I had been standing in a pretty large shadow for a lot of years and had/have more work to do then I'd realized. I have received help and support from fans, friends and musicians, from surprising corners, and from many folks who wanted nothing in return but the joy of watching someone pursue something they love at all costs.

Everyone loves a high wire act. I suppose I do as well. I started playing shows last March, and I didn't even know who I was let alone what I was going to play. I met musicians, new and old friends, fans around the country and found some things I didn't even know I had lost or was looking for.

I found a little piece of me I'd lost on the way to being what other folks needed me to be.

I found out that I am New Orleans through and through.

I was raised on First and Constance surrounded by parades and people. The St. Joseph's Day Parade went right by my house. At Mardi Gras, Pete Fountain's Half-Fast Marching Club went through my neighborhood. Music has permeated my existence from the womb like it does for anyone born in New Orleans.

I dig being on the road with all of its experiences like rafting, skiing, hiking the Grand Canyon and riding horses, but the truth is, my wife is the adventurous one and brings me along on all of those kinds of moments, moments I wouldn't have dreamed of living without her. I wouldn't have done any of it if she hadn't come on the road. I would have stayed in my hotel room for a decade with my guitar, a "Sad Poet Boy 1st Class" as my old friend Roger Manning used to say. Me, I'm strictly pavement. I like to live where I can walk or ride my bike to my favorite coffee shops in the morning and clubs in the evening. I like not getting in my car unless I absolutely have to. I like seeing people I know on the street and talking to the ones I don't. It's so good to be home, to be back in New Orleans. It's a little different but some friends and I are doing our part to make it familiar and fun, to make the New Orleans WE remember. Then it can become the New Orleans it will become...it's just going to have to get used to us tagging along.

I have spent the last month in the studio with a lot of those friends, and it's been one of the most gratifying experiences of my life. I've made records before, but I've never poured this much of me into a recording experience. I want these records to be a new start down an old path. Working with someone as talented as Ivan Neville is humbling, listening back to him playing my songs brings them to another level. Raymond Weber, not just the best drummer I ever played with, but the greatest laugh ever.

I was in a bank line last week, everyone quiet and bank-like when I heard the unmistakable, gravelly voice of James Andrews calling out "Hey Paul," like he does whenever he sees me now. It's like the voice of New Orleans saying welcome home.

I have a lot more work to do in become a working business; maintaining a career is harder then launching one, but I'm becoming actively engaged in life again and that feels great.

Today is my birthday so I guess this is my state of Paul address to anyone who reads this.

I'm having fun and learning the two main things we are put on the planet to do. Happy birthday/independence day to me.

November 2007

Po' Boy Festival, a Dancing Bee and Normalcy

The first ever Po' Boy Festival has just been held and it was a big hit with the locals.

It seems the most New Orleans of festival ideas ever and I can't believe it was the first. Who doesn't like a po' boy? The street was packed with people who came to eat, and the eating was good. Roast duck, turkey with cranberry, roast beef, portobello mushroom, barbecue shrimp. Any po' boy you could want was there, and it was a shameless eat-fest.

There were people in costume, including a girl working for the festival who was wearing a bee costume and taking time out from work to dance to the bands playing the festival. I dove in, waited in line, saw lots of folks I knew, heard music, sang (out of time) with Shamarr Allen's band and went home to pass out by 7pm.

It was a good time like I remember it. Not looking over our shoulders to make sure it was real, we were all digging it and doing what comes naturally to us here, having a good time. It's our birthright as New Orleanians.

So here's to tomorrow, moving on, and not looking back. Here's to remembering the laughter (never forgetting the hurt), and laughing that much more. Here's to music on a Monday night, drinking one too many, getting too little sleep and loving the feeling of being too tired to do anything else and then doing something else. Here's to po' boys, sno-balls, cocktails in go cups and music in the street. Summers too hot to dance and dancing anyway. Here's to winters so mild you can wear shorts and flip flops at Mardi Gras.

Here's to New Orleans.

What are we talking for? Let's have a cocktail.

December 2007

Where Else Would I Live

I am New Orleans in my heart and this is where I live.

I live in a neighborhood called the Marigny; it's across Esplanade from the Quarter and made up largely of Creole cottages, though there are some larger homes as well. It is also where you can find Frenchmen Street and if there exists in this country a magical place where beauty, innocence, decadence and poetry are available simply by opening eyes, ears and hearts, then Frenchmen is that place. The magic isn't only at night and the music isn't only in the bars. On our street here in the heart of downtown New Orleans are the usual characters of this city. Artists, business people, drunks and harmless loonies comprise just about any neighborhood in town and I have my share.

We also have Mr. Okra and the goat.

The goat is a pet of a neighbor a few doors down. He is brown and squat. He gets taken for walks on a leash and has many friends and enemies among the neighborhood dogs. He ignores their barks and struts with the dignity of a sage. In the evenings when his owner is sitting out on the porch visiting, the goat gets to roam the block. It seems so oddly perfect to see a goat wandering toward me from the direction of the Quarter as a mule drawn carriage goes clop-clopping by.

Then there is Mr. Okra who is a daily presence on the surrounding streets. Our mayor has gone missing but Mr. Okra is there for you every day. Mr. Okra drives a red pickup truck piled high with produce. His truck is hand painted, likely by Mr. Okra himself, in a style that were it not on a produce pickup truck, would sell for big money as folk art. Mr. Okra has a loud speaker that crackles as he calls out in that unmistakable New Orleans sound, "I GOT ONIONS, I GOT GREENS, I GOT PEEEEACHES." Often he will get a call on his cell phone, forget to turn off the mic, and you get to hear bits of his conversations with a family member or friend. I hear him coming and going for blocks and it makes me glad I live here. Sometimes Shelly and I will run down to buy something from him just because it's a smile. Usually seeing Mr. Okra is enough to remind me that from K-Ville to Tennessee Williams, you don't have to look far to see something so strange that if you write about it even the locals will say it's not real.

Yesterday the city went the extra mile.

We were riding bikes around the Marigny and a few blocks away heard the unmistakable call of Mr. Okra. As we got closer I heard him calling out but there was a different rhythm. He wasn't calling out alone. In a window of one of the larger houses on the block was a fellow, very inebriated, calling back. He was wearing a fedora, red velvet jacket, no shirt and was wrapped in a red velvet curtain so long and large that it blocked any view of the interior of the house, giving the scene the look of a stage play. Mr. Okra called, "I GOT ONIONS." He called back, "I GOT WHISKEY." Mr. Okra answered, "I GOT GREENS." Mr. Red Velvet Jacket called back, "I GOT VODKA." Mr. Okra called, "I GOT PEEEEACHES" and Mr. Red Velvet Jacket answered, "I GOT DRUUUUNK LAST NIGHT AND I STILL AM."

That night we drove out to Bayou St. John to have dinner. It's just a short five minute drive out to City Park but we joke about how far it is and not being able to walk or ride bikes there, which is one of our rules for socializing, "Can we ride our bikes to it?" We were meeting friends and they live on the bayou. As we arrived we heard the sound of a saxophone playing in the night. Sure enough down by the bayou, on the old footbridge by Cabrini High School, was someone playing saxophone in the moonlight. Shelly, who had been so scared to come home after the flood that I thought we'd never live here again, turned to me, smiled and said, "Where else would I live?"

The weather is warm, it's December, the windows are open and there is a Mr. Okra in the world to remind me everyday why I live here.

December 2007

'da Night before Krissmas

t'was 'da night before Kriss'mas and all through New Awhlins
every bartender's stirring Merry Krissmas to ya dahlin'.

'da bar's been set up on 'da front porch wit' care
in hopes dat a second line soon would be dere'.

'da kids pretend sleepin' up in deir beds
while visions of crawfish pie danced in deir heads.

When out on 'da neutral ground arose such a drumming
I sprang up to see if a parade was coming.

Away to google eart' I clicked in a beat,
zoomed in on my shuttahs and on to my street.

den what to my wondering eye should appear but a red pickup truck
Mistah Okra drove here.

His eyes how 'dey twinkled his bullhorn it crackled
as he called out "I HAVE ONIONS, TOMATO-O-O-ES AND APPLES."

He had homemade jams and strawberry jelly.
I ran down to 'da street to buy some for Shelly.

I heard 'da Pie Lady comin' as he drove out of sight.
wit' all 'dis eatin' and drinkin', I'm'a sleep 'til Krissmas night.

Merry Kringle, a Gear New Year, a Happy Mardi Gras and the Bestest Jazz Fest ever.

The pie lady

January 2008

That was a Fun Tune Up, Now on to Mardi Gras

I realize that most of the country is exhausted, exhilarated and ready to get back to work in the New Year. That's sweet. You may even pause now and again to feel badly for us and our struggles here in New Orleans.

Thanks, we still need tons of help, but really it's Mardi Gras season already and we're getting ready. New Year's Eve was a nice, easy warm up to the party that is the Gras.

How can I explain the difference between the lovely floats of the Rose Bowl Parade with its happy, smiling people on the float waving to happy, smiling people on the streets? It's pretty, but where's the buzz? The excitement of the Gras is catching stuff from the float riders and bringing home piles of worthless, beautiful junk/treasure. How can you really get down and dance to the marching bands going by when drinking in public is illegal? Dancing to the marching bands while carrying a beer is an art form itself, and a beautiful one if you catch it in the right light, let's say the light of a flambeaux carrier who is dancing along with you. With all respect to the Rose Bowl folks and their very beautiful parade, I like a little funk with my fun.

New Year's Eve in New York City, I've done it, also good, clean fun. With all due respect, the tradition of gathering for hours in Time Square so you can watch the Ball drop for one minute is a really fun tradition. It's fun to stand amid a sea of celebratory humanity and feel one with hope, but if you throw in some brass bands, a second line, an all night party of music in every neighborhood and you've got a party with a kick. Midnight is no time to call it a night; it's time to hit Frenchmen Street, or Tip's or wherever your favorite bands and friends will be until an hour that makes getting up for the next day, so you can begin doing the Gras again, an heroic act that is indeed celebrated with a round of applause by the friends who greet you at that event.

Mardi Gras is part celebration and part endurance test. Even fun requires pacing. Something we grow up understanding in New Orleans is that when it comes to partying, pace yourself.

Of course our pace may be a bit more than you're used to, so the second rule for a good time in New Orleans is to eat more than you think you should, drink more then you normally would, stay out way later then you ever have and take a nap after lunch.

Unless you're reading this from some place warm like Belize, you may be freezing your ass off. One more reason to come to New Orleans for Mardi Gras. Even if it's cold for us it won't be cold for you and you can laugh at us for dressing warm or laugh along with us, as long as we're all laughing.

My friend Colman deKay and me celebrating Mardi Gras

January 2008

Mardi Gras, House Concerts, Muggings and Music

Mardi Gras begins soon in my neighborhood with the march of Krewe De Vieux, the most wonderfully hilarious, politically correct/incorrect Krewe of the season. Fun. Fun. Fun.

Shelly and I were going for a bike ride to see New Orleans blues/folk icon, Spencer Bohren play at the Danny Barker Birthday Festival in the French Market. As Shelly and I stepped out of our place, our downstairs neighbor who was washing his car said, "Did you hear about the mugging?" We hadn't and asked who had been mugged. "Me. Monday night across the street from here some kid ran up and put a gun to my chest and said give me your wallet, right on that corner. I said I didn't have my wallet on me which I didn't because I was just walking my mother-in-law to her car. He ripped a necklace off my mother-in-law and ran." We asked if he was okay, he said he was and we walked on but neither of us spoke. We walked in silence both lost in thought. We're aware of how bad the crime is in New Orleans but this was across the street from us and happened at nine o'clock in the evening.

We were walking to pick up my bike at Michael's Bicycle on Frenchmen. It was two-thirty in the afternoon and there was already a great jazz band playing across the street at the Spotted Cat. The weather was fine, the music made me pause. I was already beginning to remember why we put up with the crime and other hurdles we face on our way back to home and whole. I got my bike and we began riding to see Spencer. I got bathed in music pouring from every corner, doorway and alley. Jazz bands, kids in the street, bands playing for the Danny Barker celebration, music everywhere and I felt cleansed and reminded of why I live here in the City that Care Forgot. That was the nickname for New Orleans before the flood. Back then it meant we had no cares, but now it's a hugely ironic and appropriate nickname to stick with.

What can I say, I dig it here. What looks crazy from a distance makes sense when you're dancing in it, when you are in the midst of a New Orleans moment (if you have to ask what that is then you haven't had one).

If the ride over hadn't soothed me, listening to Spencer Bohren play would have. Finger picking like a folk master and telling the story of the traditions behind the songs he played. Explaining their origins and how the songs endured.

To endure, that is what we reach for now. We endure the frustration for the moments when we can look at each other and just smile.

I've said it before but where else would I live?

You really have to see Krewe De Vieux for yourself. Grab a costume, a cocktail and a convenient excuse for work and come to Mardi Gras.

Mardi Gras Shelly

February 2008

What's Up Doc?

Passed out on Frenchmen Street during a Boutté show.

I was talking to someone on the set break and the room seemed to get hotter and hotter. I was dizzy and felt like the place was closing in on me. I went to the sidewalk thinking some air might help but the same sinking feeling told me to get as near to pavement as I could because that's where I was headed.

Woke up surrounded by my wife and a couple of shocked friends looking down at me. Again with the throwing up (this time in public), and so wiped I couldn't walk. A generous friend with a big backseat was parked nearby. He flew in like Superman and got me into his car without all of the Marigny seeing what a mess I was. He drove Shelly and me home and helped her get me upstairs. I'm sure I made a mess of his car and equally sure I will never hear a word about it from him.

Wasn't drunk, don't know what happened. I knew it was time to listen to Shelly and go to a doctor.

The doctor ran some tests and, in a way that seemed brutally casual to me, said I had a seizure disorder, most likely caused by head trauma. He said it was controllable by medication but I'd be on it the rest of my life, and it might make me a bit tired a lot of the time. He also said I couldn't drive for six months until I was seizure free or I would be criminally negligible should I be in an accident.

He said this all briefly, casually, as I say. In his view it was good news because it could have been worse and I suppose I should be grateful, but the sentence changed everything I thought I could do with my life for the next year at least and likely for the rest of my life.

I know I will figure it out but for now I am at a loss. I don't know what is next or what to expect.

Just trying to keep my hustle alive.

February 2008

Feathers

Emily Dickinson once wrote, "Hope is a thing with feathers." Woody Allen, in a sort of answer, titled a book of his, "Without Feathers".

Well, if hope is a thing with feathers then I'm not without feathers but I am a wet feather boa at the end of a rainy Mardi Gras Day.

Life is now a walk or a bike ride away and that is different. Running errands is on a schedule now or getting a lift from a friend who is off work (who is off work?). I'm getting used to it. As I wrote to my friend Chris Rose recently, I've learned in the last few years that the faster you learn to play the changes, the sooner it becomes a new song.

So I'm not without feathers though I am beat, dog tired and for the first time in my life, I can't just work as hard as possible to make things better. I have to learn to accept life's new pace, to learn some patience and to find that new path to the waterfall. I still believe in tomorrow, I'd just like it to get here so I know where I fit in.

That isn't just my story; it's the story of thousands here in New Orleans. If you've lost your house, your stuff, your job, your friends and all the routine that made up your life, where is your you-ness? Where is our we-ness? I don't know if it makes sense unless it's your life but if you lose everything that makes up your life, whose life are you living? I suppose that's what I'm trying to figure out. What is this new life I'm living? There it is again, that whole patience thing. When I figure out where I am I'll be the first to let me know.

Chris Rose wrote in the Times Picayune recently, "They love us. Almost as much as we love us. Because they have danced at the center of the universe. And once you do that, you are changed forever."

So here I am, a wet feather boa at the end of a rainy Mardi Gras day waiting for the next song so I can "dance at the center of the universe."

February 2008

Pick Yourself Up, Dust Yourself Off, Start All Over Again

I'll admit to having let things get me down lately and having those feelings come out in my writing and in conversations. I was working as hard as I could to make a new beginning in my life, and coming to terms with my health condition took the wind out of my sails for a few weeks.

I went to Memphis with John Boutté to perform at the Folk Alliance Festival. On the way to the airport, we were talking and I told him how frustrated and depressed I'd been, wondering how I would make a living without being able to drive and with ongoing health concerns. I got emotional and said, "I don't know how I'll get along in the world." Boutté raised an eyebrow, and when Boutté raises an eyebrow the sarcasm implied is second only to when my wife Shelly raises an eyebrow. He looked right at me and simply said, "Helen Keller did it." Shut me up on the spot and reminded me that I'd been feeling sorry for myself. Then he looked at me and sang the jazz standard, "Pick yourself up, dust yourself off, start all over again." As Doctor John says, "dere it is."

The Folk Alliance Festival in Memphis was like a rebirth for me. I was surrounded by acoustic instruments, songwriters and singers. People jamming, smiling and sharing. The coolest vibe I've ever experienced at a festival, and I did dozens in my years with Cowboy Mouth. I felt like I'd finally found my people, my place, and a place for my music. I can't say enough how it swept away my blues to watch others sing and play great songs with great passion, and for them to dig me doing the same. I felt as happy as a child and wished I was staying for the weekend; next time I will.

For now it was on to St. Louis to play a House Concert for my biggest champions the Gerstners and Sheltons. I'm breathing again and opening my eyes to remember that I'm surrounded by people who are pulling for me, as a person and performer.

I'm a lucky man to have the faith of many to sustain me when I doubt and stumble. The health thing isn't going away, but my pity party is over. I'm alive, I have two new records coming out, mine and

John Boutté's. There are plenty of shows to play. The life I've always wanted to live is only just beginning.

So this here wet feather boa is ready to "pick myself up, dust myself off, and start all over again." Let the music play. As Chris Rose wrote, I'm ready to "dance at the center of the universe."

I'll see you on the dance floor.

With John Boutté

March 2008

Celebrating the Life of Maw-maw Moore

Her name was Lucille but if you met her more than once her name was Maw-maw. Didn't matter if you were related, that's just what folks called her. She was born and raised in the Irish Channel around the corner from where my mom was raised. They made them tough in the Channel back then, and the music and accents from other countries were still in the voices of parents or grandparents. When I met Maw-maw, I heard in her accent the sound of my childhood, the sound of being called home. Her voice comforted me.

Maw-maw was my wife Shelly's grandmother and I was lucky to have known her. She taught me so much about love and the strength it takes to live love every day. She taught me to never take love for granted but to remember to always be grateful for its presence in your life, even on the tough days.

Fourteen years ago Shelly borrowed $3,500 from her parents to start a merchandise company for Cowboy Mouth. Maw-maw was our mailing department for the next twelve years of her life until the flood took her home, computer and all the t-shirts and discs that were in her house. When I'd go by to visit she would show me notebooks full of records of who had paid, who owed the band money, who was a good repeat customer. She would reward good customers with the occasional free poster or autograph when she thought their purchases warranted special treatment.

Once many years ago when Rob Savoy was playing bass for the Mouth, we stopped by to pick up some stuff. Maw-maw was always excited to show the band how well she kept records and how hard she worked for them so she pulled out one of her notebooks full of records. Rob, who was always quick to joke and was just being funny, pointed out that one of the checks was NSF. With her unmistakable New Orleans accent she said, "I checked on him dahlin', he's a student and I tol' 'im, baby, I know times is tough but you got to pay 'da boys fi' dollahs a mont' until you pay off 'da record and t-shirt you bought." She had him on a payment plan! Rob laughed and hugged her but she was serious, somebody owed the band money and she was tracking them down. She was seventy-eight and still plugged in to life and business.

Maw-maw loved to play cards. Many of my rock n' roll friends who sat down at a card table with the innocent looking white haired lady for a friendly game soon found themselves stared down over a dangling cigarette by a serious card player playing serious cards. More than one lost money, or if they were good enough to take her in a close hand, felt a punch on the shoulder before being complimented with "Well played baby."

From the time I met her fifteen years ago Maw-maw smoked every day. An old Mouth fan recently remarked that he always used to wonder why Mouth t-shirts smelled like smoke when a new one arrived. For awhile, we all tried to get her to stop, but she had outlived her husband Lou, most of her friends, was in her seventies, independent and continued to do as she pleased.

I used to live a few blocks away from her before the flood and would to go visit for coffee. It was strong and usually a day old, but served with such love I always went back, to get online, do band business, but mostly just to listen to her talk. I missed those visits more than I missed my house after the flood.

At first Maw-maw moved in with Shelly's Mom and Dad, but she had been on her own her whole life and couldn't stand the thought of being a burden. When I first saw her after the flood she didn't even talk, just sat in the corner in deep sadness saying her life was over. But they made them tough in the Channel. She decided to move into an assisted living center on the North Shore to be near her daughter, son and other family. This woman who was New Orleans through and through, who had been born here, married here, buried her husband here and planned to die here, became a very happy North Shore resident. She loved to gamble and found some new friends to hit the casinos with. I'm not a gambler but I did dig watching her get mad at the slots or cheer them as the moment allowed. She took her gambling to heart, even if it was for nickels.

I loved that she was never put off by my being too direct or opinionated, because I have been on occasion and needed someone with the grace to overlook it while I learned to love and trust them.

I loved that she always reminded me that love was better than anger, even when one of us was angry. I loved that happy or sad, right or wrong, she always let me know she loved me.

On Sunday, March 2nd, Maw-maw went gambling with Shelly's folks, won a few bucks on the slots. She had a nice dinner, with three deserts, before going home to sit in her rocker and enjoy her cigarette. A peaceful end to a full life.

Love, strength, honesty and commitment to the people and things you love in life. These are among the many gifts I received from knowing Maw-maw.

Maw-maw Moore

March 2008

More on Exit to Mystery Street

The title track of my latest CD, *Exit to Mystery Street*, started as an idea from my friend Colman deKay. Colman is a screenwriter from Los Angeles and has come down to New Orleans for many years for Jazz Fest. He originally had the idea to write the song with a musician friend from L.A., Gary Stockdale, who is an amazingly talented player, singer and writer (and whose name is etched in Colman's heart and mine even if it's not on the credits of the song). Gary didn't make it to Jazz Fest last year, and as Shelly was working on a television show, Colman and I hung out a bunch.

We wrote 'Exit to Mystery Street' about an experience Colman had with a young lady that bordered on the supernatural, so he says, though there is mention of shrooms, of which I know nothing. Writing with him gave me a chance to dig into my drunken bachelor past, and it was fun to write a nasty bar song again having been happily married for fourteen years. Colman got to hear me play it during Fest last year and that was cool but mostly because the song sounded like home to me. It sounded like Frenchmen Street, and I wanted to make a record that sounded like coming home.

It got me to thinking, writing and calling all of my favorite players in town to come be a part of the *Exit* sessions.

The drummer on this and every song is Raymond Weber, and it all started with the way Raymond swings a kit, laughs and swings a kit while laughing. His drumming is New Orleans and that was the start I was looking for.

The bass player was Matt Perrine who decided to play tuba on this cut which was the first of many comedic and mock serious freak-outs from our great producer Dave Pirner. Dave is not from New Orleans, he is from Minneapolis. He came down years ago looking for a drummer and found a life. He loves New Orleans but the budget was tight and I was running a lot of cats through the doors to make music as fast as I could. Fortunately they all knew each other and there was a nice reunion vibe on most of the sessions with folks catching up even though I said my hellos while running from room to room.

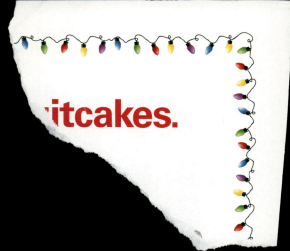

On 'Exit To Mystery Street' with Matt on tuba and Ivan Neville having played organ, Dave thought we were done. I said "No, I have a couple of horn players coming in." Dave hrumphed and went outside for a cigarette. He is a sweet fellow and never once lost his temper in the studio, but like most lead singers he is used to being listened to and sometimes I was just hearing New Orleans things that I couldn't explain, he didn't get and I wouldn't give up on so he would hrumph, go have a ciggie and come back ready to hear what madness we had conjured while he was gone, which almost always tickled him anyway.

Big Sam of Big Sam's Funky Nation came in with his trombone and Dave gave me a suspicious look, one I would come to welcome. Dave has a very dry sense of humor. Slight sarcasm, which he pulls off well because he's a funny guy but he also uses his humor to make a point, and making a joke/point he said "So-o-o-o are there parts or are we just going to noodle?" I explained that Sam knew the tune and was going to roll with it. Sam went out in the booth and George Ortolano, the engineer, asked on the intercom if Sam was ready. Sam was and they rolled. As the song played, Dave and George huddled over the board waiting for whatever Sam was going to play. Sam casually took out his trombone from the case and began to polish it. The two exchanged wide-eyed looks as the song ended and Sam called out, "That was cool, let's take another pass." By this time they were looking at each other saying "Another pass? He didn't play on the first pass." They rolled again and Sam did what Big Sam does, he pulled out a plunger and on the downbeat made that trombone cry and beg. You almost heard it ask the bartender for a shot of whiskey. Dave did something that would become familiar throughout the sessions, he pulled his bucket hat over his eyes until all you could see was a big smile and he said, "O.K., I get it."

When Shamarr Allen arrived with his trumpet to play Dave said, "You're ki-i-i-idding me, another horn player? The track is cool." I said, "It's about to be mo' cool." Not really trusting me now, he spoke out of the side of his mouth in a perfect rock sneer but with that wonderfully polite Midwestern twang softening his wariness and said mock-seriously, "mo-o-o-ore noodling?" Being possessed of a dry sense of humor and no small amount of sarcasm myself, I said, "Well Dave, down here we call it jazz, and yes, the trombone is going to speak. The trumpet will answer and the conversation between them will grow and get more exciting until the song ends." He tilted the buckethead hat back in disbelief, threw up his hands and said, "Go ahead, go crazy. What time does St. Aug's band get here?"

Shamarr listened once to what Sam and Ivan had laid down and, like a great horn player does, he went back through and hit the moments that were waiting for him, answering the call of Sam's trombone like trumpets and trombones have been doing together since wind started, going from lungs to lips and through the bells of horns until again the bucket hat came down, the smile on the face of the producer from Minnesota, "O.K. I get it."

I hope y'all dig *Exit to Mystery Street*. I poured the last six months of my life, all of my money (and an awful lot of other people's money) and my central nervous system into it.

* * *

'Door Poppin' was the first song we recorded for the Exit Sessions.

It's a song I wrote with John Boutté and his cousin Vance Vaucresson. It started like many songs that I've written with a Boutté start, with something he said. He said, "Baby we gotta write a song 'bout my sister one day, she was the 'hey now door poppin' queen of the Tremé." Well, I had no idea what he was talking about, but he went on to explain that door poppin' is "when you are so nosy you stick your face in the screen door until you pop it out", and then when she saw somebody she knew she would call out, "Hey now", which made her the hey now door poppin' queen of the Tremé. It seemed obvious to me that it was a great idea for a song.

John's cousin Vance Vaucresson supplied the Creole lyrics on the bridge. His family is fifth generation sausage makers in New Orleans; if you've ever had sausage at Jazz Fest chances are it was Vaucresson Sausage. Vance is also a singer and a song writer. At one point when John was distracted by some friends who had shown up unexpectedly, I asked Vance what the old timers in the Tremé would say about a gossipy sister you were trying to make stop. Vance thought for a moment, smiled and said, "My ma mere ti na wit' her movaison making ma cho ca over fresh ton ton." I said "That's perfect! What does it mean?" Vance explained that it means, my little sister with her gossipy mouth causing trouble (shit) over French bread (as in having the end piece of French bread with your coffee in the morning).

That is New Orleans in a short verse, a New Orleans you can smile about, a New Orleans you can sing along with, it is hanging out with John Boutté in his New Orleans.

Ivan Neville came into the studio to join Raymond on drums, Matt on bass, Sonia on electric guitar and me on acoustic. He laid New Orleans on that song without ever getting in the way. It was a joy to watch him tear through and play a solo on a song he hadn't heard before he walked in. Raymond's drumming swings the track and everybody hops on for a ride, while Ivan's playing on the B3 skips and dances all over the track.

Hope ya'll dig it.

* * *

Exit to Mystery Street and John Boutté's new record *Good Neighbor* have occupied my heart and time for the last six months. They are out in the world now and I hope ya'll dig them.

Good Neighbor is another song written with Colman deKay, my buddy from L.A., and our friend Gregory Menoher.

The song was written in John's kitchen in the Tremé as he was beginning to renovate a Boutté family home, the home of his Mamou. He was planning on living there and overseeing renovations on his mother's house next door which was a slab house and had taken a lot more water then Mamou's house had. Most of the neighborhood was being torn down or renovated and we started talking about what kind of neighbors John would get. John was in a silly mood and said well whoever moves in next door I'll make sure they get personal care. We all let our nasty blues imaginations runaway with us and came up with the idea for 'Good Neighbor'.

Once we had the framework of the song, John, who is a restless Creole Peter Pan, said we should finish it in the park. "Baby, it's too beautiful a day to waste it inside, now you get your nose out of the guitar long enough to get your ass over to the park so we can play some bocce ball." John, Colman, Gregory and I hopped on our bikes, bought a nice bottle of red wine and went to Washington Square Park on Frenchmen Street to play bocce in the setting sun. Wine cups in one hand and bocce ball in the other, we played, laughed, drank, made up lyrics, drank some more and finished the game, the song and the wine all at about the same time.

We may have been a bit tipsy and silly by then; most of the lyrics we came up with at the end of the game were too nasty to make the record but if you see John live he may sneak them in on you, so to speak.

That's how we finished the song 'Good Neighbor'.

My thanks to the Threadheads all over the world who helped make this record possible.

John and me playing at a Threadhead 'patry'

Vance Vaucresson

March 2008

d.b.a. and John Boutté

I played John Boutté's normal seven to ten set at d.b.a. because he was performing in Minnesota.

I was honored to be backed that evening by Leroy Jones, one of the finest trumpet players in New Orleans or anywhere, and Peter Harris on bass. Peter and I have worked together through John but this is the first time he backed me and he stretched my tunes in the way I've heard him do countless nights as I listened to him play with John. Leroy Jones is, simply put, a master of his instrument. Shamarr Allen is a big fan of Lee's work and he says, "Every time I think I heard Leroy play the best stuff I ever heard, he makes up new stuff. Leroy's always pushing the envelope." 'dere it is.

While I was honored they agreed to back me, I must be humble enough to admit that it was only when Boutté announced from the stage at d.b.a. the week before that he would be out of town and I would be playing, that we looked at each other with surprised faces and all quickly agreed to be a band for the night. They are gracious men and I delighted in what they brought to my songs, so I hope they dug what take I bring to the songs they play regularly.

Exhilarating to feel connected to so much creativity.

March 2008

I offer my thanks for the ongoing, gentle reminders that life goes on and that how we handle the changes determines the quality of our lives.

Some have come in e-mails, some in person, and the best by example.

Fate is kind like that.

March 2008

Ogden Museum, Tennessee Williams, Guy Fiore and Tift Merritt

What a week.

On Thursday morning I went to WWOZ with my new friend, Libra, who was representing the Ogden Museum. OZ was cool enough to play three of my tunes from *Exit to Mystery Street* on that show.

I then left OZ and attended a songwriting seminar given by Grammy nominated writer Tift Merrit as part of the Tennessee Williams Festival.

Went straight from there to the Ogden Museum to play in a beautiful atmosphere to folks who respect art and artists enough to listen and to allow themselves to engage as well.

In the middle of the show Guy Fiore, who is a friend from my days with the Mouth, snuck in to listen for a while. Guy is from the West Coast, an hour outside of San Francisco, and owns a couple of restaurants there. He used to stuff us with sushi whenever we were close enough. After he'd stuff us, most of the band would sneak off for naps, but I used to like to play a few songs for Guy and his mom Penny who always came to shows with him. Penny is a sweet woman who loves her son and a lot of the same songs as I do, so I always looked forward to seeing her and singing to her. Guy has since gone on to become a celebrity chef with a traveling cooking show, which is what had brought him to New Orleans. It was sweet to see him, to remember that his journey began with his passion for food and feeding people.

A cool reminder to follow my passion and trust that the business will follow.

Friday I went to a panel discussion with Jim McCormick, a great writer and old Bourre' playing friend, and Tift Merritt. The panel discussion was moderated by Mark Hernandez, a professor of history at Loyola and a songwriter himself. It was very interesting to hear how others write and feel about themselves as writers.

That night I opened for Tift Merritt at the Parish and it was a lovely surprise to walk in and see reserved seating and candles, an atmosphere that suggested listening. She had a packed room of folks waiting to hear her sing and I don't know how many of them knew who I was, but they couldn't have been more attentive. Listening, laughing and falling hushed in all the right places and, as I said to them, even being inappropriate once or twice at the exact right time.

Jim Brock Photography © 2009

May 2008

Writers Write

For a while now, my wife Shelly has been encouraging me to try to teach song writing. She knows I love writing even more than playing, and also she wants me to do something I love with the extra time I have these days.

Things being what they are in my life, it would be nice to find a way to have an income without traveling as much. Surprisingly, most places that teach young minds prefer that teachers have degrees from accredited universities, and I got mine on stages around the world at the university of rock n' roll. I love a great song, melody and lyric. Any decade and in most styles, a great melody and lyric grabs me until the song is part of me.

I feel lost in space and time when I write songs. Nothing comes more naturally to me. I love poems, novels, films and have been asked many times to write in another medium. I have thought about it and probably will one day, but for most of my life I wanted to focus on songs. I had a secret belief that if I stayed true to song writing that I would be rewarded by writing true songs. Like Lancelot and his virginity, Samson and his hair; I thought this would be my secret strength, my gris gris.

I still believe in song writing as one of the most beautiful forms of simple expression. The business will do what it will do with your money, and some folks are harder business people than others, but the songs have a life of their own and every once in a while I meet them again out in the world.

A post card from a younger me to the present me that I am always happy to receive, even the ones that make me wince because of time, place or the poor taste of the day.

Anyway, this is supposed to be about writing, not how I feel about it, but that is sort of the point.

Writing is easy, don't make it hard. Don't think you are making great art and you just might.

Look inside yourself. What you want to say. How you want to say it is right there at the tip of your imagining. It is singing to you in your sleep. The confusion and chaos of being awake and trying to make sense can make a melody or lyric disappear in a blink.

If you're writing, try and let go of the room, the job, the desire to write. Just be; breathe and let the winds that have whispered songs for a thousand years speak to you.

Listen to a ton of your favorite music, take walks, look around, and remember that the whole world is a song and that all of life is singing it to you every second.

With Susan Cowsill and John Boutté

May 2008

'til Tomorrow

I want to land somewhere and be still for a while, home.

I like the growing distance between the band I was and the man I am.

It would be nice if I was getting paid for the songs I wrote, which the band I used to be in continues to release and re-release. Not for the money alone, though it would be nice to get paid for my work, but it would be nice for a part of my life that was so much fun to not be so dirtied by the business.

Even still, it was a fun time and more and more these days, that is what I choose to remember.

Really I've been blessed. I've traveled the world with the woman I love, having fun with people I like and playing music.

I still do, at a different pace, with a different feeling in my music and in my heart.

Shelly and me in London

May 2008

Slow Motion Notions

It's hot and steamy in New Orleans and I'm digging it.

I like leaving the a/c off, the fans on, the windows open and wearing less clothes. I like sitting still and having a breeze blowing be the most exciting moment of the afternoon. I like the slower pace that life begins to take on.

I like moving on.

I've had the chance to play some fun festivals with the Rolling Road Show and, in the true spirit of the project, it has been a different line-up for each gig. What fun hearing my songs played by so many wonderful musicians! Fun to learn the songs of the different songwriters playing with me and adding them to the set. Fun watching other folks shine while you play and groove to the energy that the union creates.

Shelly and I moved again. Sixth time we've moved since the Thing. I suppose we'll stop moving when it feels like home again or when we figure out what that is. I dig where I am, had fun where I was and look forward to where I'm going, which is all good.

What's more, summer is here and I'm not in a hurry to figure any of it out. Walk slow, play slow and don't generate body heat unless you have to.

A great time to mediate or anything else you can think of that takes less moving than you did just last week.

June 2008

Bo Knew Cool

Years ago when the Mouth was first getting started, we drove 15 hours from Jackson, Mississippi, where we played a double wide called W.C. Don's, to Charlotte, NC, so that we could open for Bo for $150.00. The thing was, the opener got to be the backing band. Bo, like Chuck Berry, uses the opener in whatever town he plays and we wanted to back Bo so we begged for the gig. He arrived and eyed us with contempt, just another white boy backing band.

During sound check, Bo went into the first song without saying the key or the title, but we were big fans for years so we knew the song. Bo waved us off after a verse and chorus. He smiled for the first time all day (he'd been scowling since he arrived), and spoke to us for the first time saying, "Ye-e-ah, we gonna have some fun tonight."

Then the promoter walked up all smiles and, wanting to take care of Bo, said, "Mr. Diddley, we have a car waiting and reservations at one of the best restaurants in Charlotte." Bo was not happy, "Restaurant? I'm tired and I don't want to go to no restaurant." The promoter was young and scared and stammered, "B-b-b-ut Mr. Diddley, it says in your contract that you require a meal after sound check!" "That's right," Bo said glaring, "I get some Church's Fried Chicken in my hotel room!" and he walked away.

Backing Bo that night was something I'll never forget. I'd played his stuff since I could play because it was easy (many of his songs are one chord), and because he rocks. Certainly nobody ever rocked one chord harder.

Bo dug us as well. He played for over two hours, even though he'd only been contracted for an hour and a half. We hung out for a while after the show, and Bo offered the best advice anyone has ever given me about playing music. He said, "I like you fellas and I'm gonna tell ya' something I want you to remember. Keep it Simple and Think of Church."

June 2008

Trying To Begin Again and Again and Again...

Occasionally when I mention the Mouth, I get e-mails from well meaning people telling me to "get over it", "stop with the sour grapes" or my personal favorite, "accept that you'll never be as successful as you were with Cowboy Mouth and go back to the band."

This isn't some broken hearted lover stuff. I've had my chance to mourn the loss of the friends we were. The songs I wrote for them and have been writing for all of my life are mine-my heart, my life, and my songs. 'Light It On Fire' was written in 1987 five years before there was a Cowboy Mouth from New Orleans. These songs were my retirement money, my walking away money, my rainy day, my travel is hard because of seizures money.

There is no pension plan in rock n' roll, you roll while you rocking. What you are left with when it's over is what you created; your music. These songs sprang from my imagination and someone else has decided to keep the money, keep my pension, my retirement. My songs, that came from me.

I'm trying to begin again and again and again.

With all of its problems, I feel happier here in New Orleans and I'm glad to be back in the city, as sweet Susan Cowsill sings, "Where I know who I am." I'll wake up here tomorrow.

I'm still in there pitching, kids, like an old pitcher with a tired arm squeezing out one more season.

Play Ball!

June 2008

What a Wonderful Weekend, Mostly

Tipitinas was beyond what I expected on every level.

I couldn't believe how many people came to the show. I was knocked out that the floor was full and there were even some folks upstairs. The Rolling Road Show was rolling as well. I learned 'I May Be Wrong' and 'Miss Tourist' from Matt Perrine's *Sunflower City* disc and really enjoyed singing them. I also learned a song from Craig Klein's disc *New Orleans Trombonisms* called 'Marie Laveu'. A lot of words to remember but now I know a classic New Orleans song with brilliant lyrics, so it was worth the effort. We also did a couple of Tin Men songs that Alex sang, 'Baby' and 'Jingling Down The Street' and of course a few from Shamarr's *Meet Me On Frenchmen Street* record which I dig so much. Big fun but I didn't get in until after two in the morning. This was to be my first weekend of touring since the cancellations caused through my illness, and I was trying not to be worried about how the old man would hold up.

On a few hours sleep I flew to Kansas City and was driven an hour to Willie's Bar in Lawrence, Kansas. It was a sweet if slightly out of control party. Three friends had flown me in for a House Concert which they decided to move to another friend's bar. One guy was celebrating because his wife had come from her baby shower, another couple was moving to New Orleans to help rebuild the city, and everyone was happy knowing life was changing. Happy for each other and a little sad about letting go. Sweet. Naturally the husbands got drunk, but I may have written a new song, 'The Fastest Drunk in the West', from the experience.

Then, on three hours sleep, I got a car service for the hour back to KC for a 5 a.m. flight to Charlotte where my buddies Phil and Joy were waiting to pick me up for the hour drive to Rock Hill for an early House Concert. The concert was a surprise for the birthday husband who was genuinely speechless, and I was touched that someone would be that pleased to hear me sing as a birthday gift. I was supposed to play an hour and a half, but you know when Bo Diddley was having fun he just kept going, and I was having fun both nights so it was two hour plus shows both times. Phil and Joy were kind enough to take me for a bite near the airport so I could catch a flight home. This was to be the nicest part of the whole experience; I was flying home to be with Shelly having only missed one night with her.

It had been a heck of a run and I could feel my energy flagging, and I dozed off on Phil once or twice on the ride back to Charlotte.

Dropped with smiles and hugs from friends at the Charlotte airport, I waited to board the flight and collapsed in my seat as soon as I could. I was awakened by a flight attendant with a slight accent. I was now groggy, a bit disoriented and about an hour and a half away from needing my second dose of seizure medicine of the day. I've spent weeks trying to get regimented about it and knew I had to take the pills on time or there would be consequences. Shelly had told me that I should take extra because "you never know", but I told her I'd be home for my pill and a hug before she went to bed.

The flight attendant who woke me asked me to turn off my ipod which I did. She woke me again, irritated that my headphones were still in. By now I was barely conscious but I held up the cord to show that it was unplugged and said, "Baby, it isn't even plugged in." This was my first mistake. Never call a woman, or a man for that matter, that you don't know outside of New Orleans, 'baby'. The attendant walked to the front of the plane in a huff. Now I'm awake, groggy, but awake, and like most middle-aged men do when they wake up, had to pee. I headed for the back of the plane where the rear attendant asked what I was doing. I told her I'd been awakened and had to pee. She didn't ask me to return to my seat, she didn't tell me not to pee, and she didn't ask if I could wait until we were airborne. When I was done, I was escorted to the front of the plane where the first flight attendant had reported me as being drunk. Now I'm off my meds, I'm barely aware and I'm trying to explain that my ipod was off. I'm not drunk, I just want to go home.

I WANT TO GO HOME.

At this point some guy sitting nearby calls out my name. I can see the guy and I know him but I can't place him. I'm thinking someone from the music scene, and think that maybe he'll help explain about the 'baby' thing. Really, I called my father-in-law baby and he is about six foot four and built like a tank. Normally folks from New Orleans will try to help each other out, but for some reason this guy calls out my name again and he's pissed. He's glad they're taking me off the plane.

Right then, I know I'm not going to make my flight or my next dosage and will be at risk for a seizure for a day or two until I can get back on schedule. So I'm a bit panicked and I explain all of this to the Terminal Supervisor who says yes, she can see I'm not drunk, I'm articulate and she will put me on the next flight. At this point airport police arrive.

It's all over, I'm off the plane, the supervisor has determined that I am no trouble to fly on the next flight and the airport cop in charge breaks in on the conversation. I try to say that all I need at this point is my ticket, but suddenly I'm being shoved in the chest by the guy in charge, a blond, shaved/crew cut, blue eyed cop. I mean I'm either in George Bush's America or I've traveled back in time and might finally get to meet Anne Frank. Either way, I'm further from New Orleans then I've been in a long time, in every way possible.

I wonder about that flight attendant and that guy who knew my name. I wonder if they have ever known illness or have known it in someone they loved. I wondered if the blonde cop with the shaved head might have loved someone who had a condition, or would he not care and just like the chance to kick some ass because he's young, jacked up and trained to.

I wonder how I suddenly feel so frail and tired. I wondered why I would leave Shell for a second to go through this.

June 2008

Lessons

I usually say I'm self taught on guitar, but this isn't quite true.

One of my older brothers, Andrew, was a good guitarist when he was young and he gave me a few lessons, but I was always racing past the lesson trying to get to the song. I was fourteen when he taught me.

My mom paid for the guitar at Campo's on Broad Street. Mom didn't have the money for something like that but my sister's boyfriend, Dan, who had a good job at WWL-TV selling advertising, co-signed for my mother on a payment plan so I could get the guitar.

When I got a bit better on the guitar, Dan, who became my brother-in-law, also taught me to play my first rock n' roll songs. Buddy Holly songs, showing me how to hic-cup like Buddy did when he sang. Elvis songs, showing me how to moan like Elvis. He taught me how to sing harmony like the Everly Brothers. These weren't lessons, at least he never made it feel like that, this was just two guys hanging out strumming. Well, really it was one guy hanging out waiting for his date to finish getting ready and teaching me guitar was safer by a mile than trying to talk to my mother.

I banged on the guitar through high school and an honorable mention should go to my cousins, the Burkes, who I lived with in my sophomore year of high school. I was learning to play and sing my first song, 'Proud Mary'. It took me the whole first semester to get it done and it must have seemed like a whole year to them, but they never complained. They were a family of athletes, the oldest sister became a nun, their father was a politician and their mother a tireless fund raiser for the Catholic Church. They weren't annoyed, though they had every right to be because I was quite terrible for the first week or two. They weren't annoyed because they each in their own way understood that discipline and practicing the guitar may have been the first sign of discipline that anyone in my family had ever seen in me.

Never got girls with the guitar, but my friends liked for me to play because girls would come around, and while I was caught up in singing, my friends would make new friends. When I'd open my eyes at the end of the song my audience would have vanished to a nearby car or empty field.

I took guitar briefly in college in an ill-fated attempt to become a serious musician. Jimmy Robinson was my instructor first semester. Jimmy is a founding member of the legendary New Orleans fusion rock band Woodenhead, and he also plays in one of the most mind blowing collection of guitar talents in town called Twangorama. He is also one of the kindest musicians I've ever worked with, which surely explains the only passing grade I was to receive in classical guitar.

Now 28 years later, I'm taking lessons again.

I'd come to accept long ago that I had limitations on the guitar, and that I was more of a songwriter. I have said many times over the years to friends, fans and musicians that I hire, "I write the songs and get real players to play them." Usually got a big laugh and everybody is generally cool with letting you run your own session even if it involves you not playing on your own songs. I used this line with Alex McMurray recently when he asked if I wanted a solo on any of the songs in the set. Alex isn't from New Orleans, he's from New Jersey. In New Orleans we embellish or outright sling bullshit for fun and your friends go "yeah baby, 'dat's right". As I say, Alex is from Jersey and he didn't laugh, he smiled with his head tilted, a little confused by the thought and finally said, "Yeah, that's one way of doing it I suppose."

I'd wanted to take lessons from John Rankin for years and I was determined to seek him out. Naturally, I didn't because insecurities about my playing and my ability to learn to play better (careful of the bullshit you fling, some may stick with you) kept me from doing so, as they had many times through the years I was with the Mouth. As it turns out, John heard me speak about song writing at the Tennessee Williams Festival and he came to me to ask about song writing lessons. We struck a bargain. I'm taking guitar lessons and looking at his songs with him. I think I'm getting the better part of the deal because John is already a fine song writer, whilst I've built a career based on my limitations as a guitar player. We call it playing primitive in rock bands. It's fun for me to work on his songs because he is mostly asking for the words to be shaped a bit which I dig doing. It's also fun because what he considers "a pretty standard blues song" has little turns of chord and notes that are new to me as a player but completely familiar as a singer/song writer/listener, so it's making connections in my head.

The lessons themselves are my favorite part. This is surprising because I only took John up on his invitation to come by because I like writing songs. I figured he'd see pretty soon that the lessons weren't going to help, but John Rankin is a great teacher and I hadn't counted on this. He focused on my strengths. We talked about songs and song writing and my love of melody as well as lyric. Then he showed me a few simple things about how to build around a melody, not to over complicate things with theory and let your voice, which knows how to sing, tell your fingers what to play without letting too much thought clutter up your expression. He told me this over several weeks and lessons, all in the simplest of terms which still left me dazed and confused. However, each week as I would practice the light bulbs started going off, and I am making more and more connections to what I'm learning and what I already know. Instead of being intimidated by the thought of soloing, I'm looking forward to it. I'm very grateful to John for my ongoing lessons and a growing friendship.

I'm also looking forward to surprising Shamarr Allen and whipping out a guitar solo on *Meet Me On Frenchmen Street*. Y'all don't tell him... I want to sneak up on him.

Shamarr Allen

Alex McMurray

June 2008

Bright Lights of Los Angeles

I am going to play a gig in Los Angeles with Shamarr Allen and John Boutté, and I wish I could have sold tickets to the rehearsal.

We scheduled for twelve so I was certain it would be a one o'clock rehearsal. I knew to call Boutté an hour and a half before because he would have forgotten (or pretended to have forgotten) about rehearsal. I knew to call Shamarr an hour before because he is young, busy, a father, has friends to keep up with and though I love him, he digs late.

Boutté answered the phone pretending to be asleep. It was eleven o'clock. I've known him for twelve years and he rarely sleeps past nine. Yawning, he said, "Rehearsal? What day was 'dat baby? Today? Let me wash my ass an' I'll be over by one." Shamarr answered, "Wassup? I'm in Baton Rouge pickin' up fliers but I'll be back by one or one thirty." Perfect, we're right on schedule.

I don't know how well some of you know John Boutté, but he is one of the slowest moving humans on the planet. I waited for him on my balcony on Esplanade and he arrived promptly late at ten after one in his giant '67 Cadillac. John is about 5 foot three inches of Creole mischief, "a bellicose Pan" as he was described by the Washington Post. Picture this small package of jazz and New Orleans history behind the wheel of such a monster. I watched him take at least a full minute to park and another, perhaps two to three minutes, to emerge from his car. He was wearing his old summer Stetson, a bright orange Hawaiian shirt, orange striped seersucker pants and bright orange (though not matching the shirt) Crocs, and was carrying his old battered trumpet case. Walking the fifty feet to my building took as long as the average person takes to go to the bank and back.

We waited for Shamarr, who I hoped wouldn't be so late that John would split before he got there, and John played some trumpet for me. We have a deal, I'm working on my guitar playing and he is working on his trumpet. Neither of us is looking for mastery, just to give a little something back to the guys that play with us. I played some songs while John showed me stuff he was working on. To watch John Boutté play trumpet is like seeing a Creole Popeye, one eye closed and face scrunched up in focus, about to burst a cheek like Dizzy Gillespie as a Looney Tunes cartoon.

Shamarr showed up a respectable twenty minutes late with his six year old son and the son of Dinneral Shavers in tow. Dinneral was a drummer for the Hot Eight Brass Band and a high school music teacher, who was shot and killed in one of the many random acts of violence that American cities are known for, and that have become all too common place here in New Orleans since the flood.

It was the first time these two guys got together and to really pay attention to each other as players and people and Boutté was clearly touched by knowing how Shamarr has cared for Dinneral Jr. since that time and by bringing him to rehearsal. I have a big balcony and the boys had a good time chilling safely out of ear shot from Boutté and his salty tongue.

One of the reasons for the rehearsal was to get a feel for how to back them both up. I've backed John up for years and Shamarr many times in the last two years but they have very different styles and I needed to feel how to back them up at the same time and make it feel like one. The other reason is that Shamarr and John have never really played a gig together besides one with me and they needed to get a feel for each other.

I had a set list ready and was set to get to work. Boutté, on the other hand, wanted to show Shamarr his trumpet work, so he was determined to play trumpet on every song we practiced. The end result being that between his Popeye face and his still becoming trumpet playing, Shamarr was laughing as much as he was playing. Boutté was playing his Popeye trumpet and not singing and I was watching my one rehearsal go by in what looked like chaos and laughter. My attempts to get Boutté to stop playing the horn and sing only resulted in louder blasts on the trumpet. Shamarr was no help at all because he likes playing the trumpet and likes teaching so he was showing John stuff and encouraging him to play more. This would have been all well and good if we had a month, but we had a week and knowing John, I knew he had no intention of playing the trumpet on a gig just yet. When John did sing, he was changing all the words so that they were dirty limericks, further frustrating my attempts at a 'serious' rehearsal.

It wasn't until later that I realized this was their way of getting to know each other. They didn't need to play the music, they are both great and would be on that night. They needed to find out what made the other cat laugh, where his heart was so they'd know where each other's music was coming from. The whole business of me trying to motivate Boutté to focus was the funniest thing of all for Shamarr. He said that we should forget about playing the Los Angeles show and try to get a reality show for me and John so folks could listen to us fuss with each other.

In the end it was a good rehearsal in that they had a sense of what to expect from each other musically, but really, I wish you could have seen it.

Playing The Joint in LA with John Boutté and Shamarr Allen

August 2008

Thanks, Blogs, Learning and Laughing

It's been three years since life went sideways. I've tried to be honest and share as much of my experiences as I could in my writing. The losses, the surprises on the road back, the road back turning into the road to somewhere else, the joy of rebirth and frustration.

I did so hoping that other folks who were going through similar experiences would remember that life is a shared journey, and smile in the remembering.

It's been three years and we're three days away from the day.

My journey has turned inward.

I plan to spend a lot of time practicing guitar and looking for new paths to the waterfall.

Thanks for listening, commenting, supporting and even disagreeing.

September 2008

Jet Black and Jealous

Life is filled with surprises.

Sixteen years after I released my solo debut disc, *Jet Black and Jealous*, on a small label out of Georgia, 'Jet Black and Jealous', the song, is being released on a major label out of Nashville.

About nine months ago I got a call from a lawyer in Nashville who said he represented a song writer and publisher in Nashville who was a fan of my work. I said, "uh-huh." He said his client had re-written a song of mine called 'Jet Black and Jealous' just for his own amusement, but that somehow, without his client the song writer knowing it, his manager had passed the song on to Universal records. I said, "uh-huh." He said, "I know, a lawyer from Nashville can't be good news?" I told him not in my experience, but asked him to continue. He said that the song was to be recorded by The Eli Young Band for their major label debut and that his client wanted to make sure I was cool with the re-write and that I got my share. I was knocked out.

Here I've been chasing down some of my beast friends to get paid for songs I'd written with and for them over fifteen years, and a stranger was calling me to make sure I liked his client's re-write and I was paid fairly for my contribution. I'd heard a lot over the years about how tough Nashville was as a business town, but I can tell you that Nashville treated me more fairly in this bit of business then anything I'd seen in rock n' roll. Well, that's not entirely true. My friends in Hootie and The Blowfish recorded a song of mine on their last studio record. The song was called 'Leaving' and they changed it around a bit when they recorded it, but made sure I got credit for the work and paid for the release.

Maybe it wasn't rock n' roll that burned me, maybe the guys I worked with and believed in for so long are just a drag.

I went to the Billboard Country Music Charts today to check on the release of Darius Rucker's record. Darius has been a friend for years since Hootie and the Mouth were in vans and trading opening gigs in the SEC club circuit. I think he has one of the most beautiful and recognizable baritone voices in music today. The cat could sing the phonebook and I'd be happy to listen. When I pulled the Billboard chart up on my computer, I was happy and proud to see that D. had made his country music debut in the #1 spot. Then I noticed that making its debut in the #5 spot was The Eli Young Band with 'Jet Black and Jealous'. I had known about the release for months but had no idea it would be the title cut. More whispers from the universe to keep on keepin' on.

Many thanks and best wishes to the Eli Young Band for recording the song and naming their record after it. I thought it was a fine title when I was young and hope they sell a few million copies.

October 2008

Do You Voodoo?

The Tenth Ritual of Voodoo Festival was recently held in New Orleans. I was there from the beginning and am glad to have played this one.

The first year of Voodoo, Shelly and I lived on Orleans Ave., just off City Park Ave. City Park was and remains my favorite place to jog to or through so I was able to watch them build Voodoo from the ground up. I could sit on my balcony and hear the music, watch the people going to and from, and it was a gas to witness the new energy it brought to my neighborhood and the city.

Stephen Rehage, who started and still runs Voodoo Fest, was kind enough to have me play there many times when I was with Cowboy Mouth.

The most unforgettable time was the Voodoo Fest he gave for free in New Orleans just one month after the flood. Shelly and I had been home once, but for most of us on the bus it was to be the first real look at New Orleans post-Katrina, and we couldn't have known what to expect. Fred was dropped off in Metairie and the rest of the band and crew rode with Shelly and me to our flooded house in Gentilly. They walked with us and experienced for themselves what the loss looked, felt and smelled like. There was nothing to salvage and we had to get to the show so we didn't linger.

As we were leaving, someone found, on a tall shelf, a baseball that hadn't flooded. Shelly had been collecting baseball memorabilia for years and the ball was signed by the LSU baseball team that had won the College World Series a few years ago (she's a big Tiger fan). Everyone smiled, glad that something had survived, that we could leave with something. Shelly, being Shelly, looked at the ball and smiled. She tossed it in the air once, caught it and threw a fastball through the glass front door that the National Guard had kicked in. Then she smiled again and said, "I always wanted to do that."

We drove from the destruction of Gentilly to the beauty and tranquility of Uptown, most of us feeling relief at the sight of undestroyed New Orleans. Our guitar tech at the time was the son of a veteran, nephew of a veteran, brother to veterans and proud of America in the most right wing of ways. Jake and I had become friends, though he would not tolerate conversations about my anger at the government "for their criminal ineptitude," as Bruce Springsteen would later say at Jazz Fest after the flood. This same Jake looked around throughout the ride in disbelief, enraged, asking over and over again, "Where is my army? Where are the soldiers I know? We can destroy a city and rebuild it in a month, what is going on here?"

It was under this cloud that we arrived at Voodoo Fest, emotionally raw, angry, frightened and uncertain. We needed to play music as much as the people in the crowd needed to hear music, and we all desperately needed to feel something besides pain. Mr. Rehage gave us all the chance to remember the best part of New Orleans; music as release, music as healing, and music as redemption.

It was one of the most memorable shows I'll ever do from a time where I'd like to forget almost everything, almost.

I live in a different part of town now, but I still make City Park part of my run so I have been watching again as they built the Voodoo Fest this week.

When I played at the festival this year, I played for my friends relocated in Texas who were hurting, my friends throughout the country who were there for me when I lost my home and now because of changing times were facing uncertain futures, lost jobs and homes themselves. I played mostly because it's fun and it makes me feel good, it makes me feel connected.

Tony Fitzpatrick, an artist and poet from Chicago wrote to me recently that he loved New Orleans because "it's a place where you can go to hurt, it's a place where you can go to heal, and it's a place where you can go to find your own dirty grace."

November 2008

Walking Through Heaven's Gate

The Glen David Andrews live gospel record was recently recorded at the Zion Hill Missionary Baptist Church in the Tremé.

I played guitar in the backing band and Glen David and I wrote a new song for the recording, 'Walking Through Heaven's Gate'. The song came about because of Glen's larger than life energy and enthusiasm. We were rehearsing for a gig and he said he wanted to write a song for his record. After being in his presence for the night, I went home as inspired as if I'd already been to a gospel show myself, which is how Glen can leave you feeling. That night I woke up at three in the morning with a song in my head. I recorded it and went back to bed. I showed it to Glen at sound check and we agreed to play it that night. At show time, he whipped a napkin out of his pocket and said he'd written a third verse and made a couple of lyric changes.

Two weeks later I was in the Zion Hill Baptist Church listening to the choir sing the song and watching the beautific smiles on their faces at the thought of "walking through heaven's gate, me and the Lord face to face." Sweet.

The rehearsals with the gospel choir and organist/choir leader were wonderful. These folks are beautiful in the sincerity of their faith. The joy they let loose when they sing is real. It was a gift to sit among them at rehearsals and to be a part of it. To hear them sing a song I had a hand in writing was chilling.

One of the reasons we live here in New Orleans are the moments of surreal beauty, odd juxtapositions of peoples, cultures and music that all blend together and create a humanity that is poetic, tragic and comic all in the same instant.

It was a night of music to lift your spirits.

With Glen David Andrews

November 2008

Thanks

I have a home again. What a simple and lovely thing to be thankful for. After three years of wandering and six different residences, we closed on a place in the Tremé.

I had thought it would be the Marigny, the streets I dance on and play my music on these days, but it's the Tremé. It makes sense to me. John Boutté, the Andrews family, the second lines I've walked and musical history lessons I've received in the last few years have been from my friends in the Tremé and now it is home.

I want to thank all the folks who cheered me on and supported me as I continue to try and make a new life in a new New Orleans.

Like so many of my friends here, the urge to want to lay down and give up was there from time to time. The feeling of wanting to disappear completely led me to Belize for a while, but home would not let go of our hearts and New Orleans is home. I was able to keep hoping because folks kept listening at shows to my songs, and through my writing, where I found a way to speak out loud to myself and make sense of the seemingly senseless. Thank you for listening.

The songs keep coming and I am increasingly blessed to have voices like John Boutté, Glen David Andrews, Shamarr Allen, Susan Cowsill, and my favorite new band, The Eli Young Band, sing tunes of mine. I'm thankful.

Most importantly, I am thankful for the love of my wife, Shelly. The thing I most feared after the flood wasn't losing my house or stuff or job. It was my love. I held on tightly these last few years so the current of the flood waters did not wash us away from each other.

Birds are singing outside my window,

Shelly is downstairs making a pot of beans.

Mr. Okra still drives by my house, my home.

I'm home, New Orleans.

Epilogue

January 2009

Down In the Tremé It's Me and My Baby

So there it is... two years of my life.

I have work happening now writing songs with a lot of different folks around town. 'Jet Black and Jealous' has been in the Billboard County Music Charts for 17 weeks and counting. There is a new disc with Boutté; we finally got around to that duo release for the Threadheads. *Stew Called New Orleans* will be coming out in the Spring, in time for Fest.

Gigs here and in other cities. Boutté and I played Canada, New York and L.A. in the last few weeks, and there are more shows on the horizon with the Rolling Road Show as well as on my own.

I've learned to communicate with other musicians and to the world again.

My songs have grown.

I feel a part of this city again, connected to life and creativity.

I have a home in the Tremé. Shelly and I love our house. It is a small, two story Creole Cottage style home. Shelly has already begun some slight renovations, building additional shutters for the side windows to match the front ones and painting them all a new color. A color she chose for the shutters of her new home. She has been doing this under the watchful eye of a very sweet, inquisitive lady from the Tremé Neighborhood Association who has politely quizzed about the shutters and color changes, while not too discreetly checking out the character of the home's new owners. I was pleased when the look of concern on her face changed to a smile followed by an invite to attend a meeting some time. Even better was finding out that this obviously powerful and presiding voice in the neighborhood, who had just given us her approval, is married to the father of Shannon Powell, the same Shannon who cooked the meal at that lake house in Ohio, the memory of which still lingers on my taste buds.

Mardi Gras is near and from our balcony we can hear the John McDonough marching band getting ready for parade season as they march around and around our block, playing their street beat and breaking into a song at every other corner. This fantastic event takes place daily outside our front door at around 4:30 in the afternoon and it has quickly become our favorite time of day to stop working, turn off the computers and television, open the windows and listen to the music flow. We are home indeed.

When we got the house, the first thing Glen David Andrews told me was, "Welcome to the Seventh Ward, you gonna see a second line now." We moved in a month and a half ago, and this past Sunday the first second line passed under our balcony. It was somber, spiritual, tragic, poetic and joyful. That is how a second line unfolds. Shelly called me to the balcony. I walked out and was surprised to see a hearse in the street below. I could hear the band coming; they were a half block away still playing a dirge as they crossed Esplanade. Once they were across they broke into a second line and it was joyful and beautiful in the way that only a real second line can be. This was no party in the Quarter, this was a funeral. Someone was being sent to Gloryland, and the folks were going to make sure there was a brass band playing with dancing on the streets of heaven and earth. There were old gentlemen in suits and Stetsons and pretty ladies in dresses and high heels.

The first song John Boutté and I ever wrote together was 'Foot of Canal Street'. We were walking down near the cemeteries at the end of Canal Street, comparing the similarities in our lives. John and I had met at the home of the song writer, Michelle Shocked, when she lived in New Orleans for a while. We had both been playing music professionally in New Orleans for over a decade at the time, but we had never met. Michelle had a gift for bringing people together who should have met, but hadn't. We found out that we were born a year apart, three days apart, both were raised in a house full of sisters and, as we walked down Canal Street, we found out we had something else in common. We were talking about the differences in our lives growing up in New Orleans in the sixties, he in the Tremé and me in the Channel, him playing jazz and me playing rock n' roll, he being black and me being white. As we reached this point in the conversation, we were about a block and a half away from a cemetery which John pointed to and said, "You know baby, my daddy's buried in that cemetery." I said, "Johnny, that's one more thing we got in common, my daddy's buried across the street." He looked at me, smiled and said, "You know what baby? Black or white, sooner or later, we all gonna meet at the Foot of Canal Street." I told him we had to write a song which said just that, so we walked back to where I was living at the time on Bienville in Mid-City to see if we could write a song together. I thought we should try and write a song that sounded like it could be played at a second line funeral. I said, "You've sung and played at second line funerals. What's it like? It looks so holy, it looks so spiritual, and it looks so beautiful." He gave a sly grin, one that I would get to know very well over the next twelve years, and said, "We-e-e-el baby. It's beautiful and all bu-u-ut you know, mostly the bitches wonder what the other bitches gonna be wearing...and the men all be carrying a flask in their hip pocket waiting for the band to kick it so they can...you know, kick it too." He said all of this laughing, thrusting hips, waving arms. Comically, serious and seriously comic, it was a song before my eyes, all I had to do was put it to music.

Now that very procession is outside my door. The women are indeed each dressed brilliantly, and the men seem somber in their black Stetsons and bowler hats, but if you watch long enough you may see someone take a little sip off a flask because after all, it is a bit damp and foggy this morning.

This is no movie folks. K-Ville got cancelled and Tennessee Williams isn't writing anymore. This is life in New Orleans, it's my life and I couldn't have lived it anywhere but here with Shelly.

We were watching the news around six this evening; the sun was just beginning to set when we heard a trumpet playing. It was kind of late for the band to be practicing and it was a lone trumpet anyway. I went the balcony to see what was up as I heard Shelly say, "It's just someone waiting for the bus," and so it was.

Nothing 'just' about living a life filled with such magical moments as these.

Boutté has a tune he wrote that I have loved for over a decade, and now I am living it. The words to the chorus are, "Hanging in the Tremé, watching people sashay, down my block, outside my house, in front of my door...down in the Tremé it's me and my baby, we're all going crazy." As Doctor John says, "dere it is."

Although the news says there are bad times ahead for this country, we here in New Orleans are here to say you will survive. We have seen the worst of what this country can be, but we've also seen the best that the people of this country can be.

People came from all over to help us rebuild when we couldn't lift our heads from crying. Folks gutted and rebuilt homes of families they will never meet, families that could never have the right words to thank them if they did meet. It is a spirit that has not, and I believe cannot be extinguished by misfortune or government apathy.

We have a new president now, and there is new hope in the country and in the city of New Orleans. We are here, we are dancing again, and we have remembered how to smile without wondering if it's the right kind of smile.

We are singing to you America. If you listen you can hear us saying that all of us fall down sometimes and that there is a tomorrow.

REBUILDING NEW ORLEANS
ONE SONG AT A TIME!

★★★★★★★★★★★★★★★★★

THREADHEAD RECORDS IS A NEW AND UNPRECEDENTED NON-PROFIT RECORD COMPANY HELPING THE MUSICIANS OF NEW ORLEANS.

IT'S SIMPLE... FANS FUND THE CDs AND THE MUSICIANS PAY BACK THOSE FUNDS PLUS 10% FOR THE NEW ORLEANS MUSICIANS CLINIC.

VISIT THE WEBSITE TO FIND OUT HOW YOU CAN HELP REBUILD NEW ORLEANS... ONE SONG AT A TIME.

www.threadheadrecords.com